Shifting Gears

Order this book online at www.trafford.com
or email orders@trafford.com

Most Trafford titles are also available at major online book retailers.

Print information available on the last page.

ISBN: 978-1-4120-5816-2 (sc)

Trafford rev. 08/02/2022

www.trafford.com
North America & international
toll-free: 844-688-6899 (USA & Canada)
fax: 812 355 4082

SHIFTING GEARS

My Global Bike Odyssey

AL YOUNG

edited by Kristine Kopperud

This book is dedicated to Elizabeth Kelly,
without whose inspiration and encouragement
I would never have taken this trip.

Contents

Acknowledgements

Many thanks to the following people:

Mary Kaufman for encouraging me to write a book and demanding details, details, details. Also, a super thanks for allowing me to use her phone card to send my daily emails home for the Webpage.

Jodi Ferguson for the first editing process.

Kristine Kopperud Jepsen for the final edit and many, many hours spent helping me.

Betty Robertson for being a loving sister, my personal sounding board and my personal nurse during my recovery phase.

Craig Carpenter for suggesting, creating and updating my personal Website; for managing my personal finances for the year; and for giving unending moral support before, during and after the trip.

Fred Rose for his belief in me and for the financial boost.

Craig Kunz for his support and wisdom. How did you know?

Dallas Beck for taking my job, living in my house and driving my car, and then giving them all back to me when I came home.

Mom and Dad for not trying to talk me out of returning to the trip after my accident. That meant a lot to me.

My friends who never doubted me for a minute.

And to all my Webpage readers for your encouragement throughout the year. It kept me going when the times got tough.

And finally, I have to add a huge thanks to the many riders on Odyssey 2000® who helped make my year the highlight of my life. I would never be complete without your friendship.

Preface

In January of 1996, my friend Craig Carpenter and I looked over the National Bicycle Association list of tours across states, highlighting the ones that would fit our schedules.

We had been cycling on our own all summer and fall, using the hub-and-spoke method of camping in one spot until we exhausted all ride options, then picking up and moving to another spot. Or we'd do day rides out of Jackson, Wyoming, or Driggs, Idaho. That was the summer I had ridden my first 50-mile ride, and I was so ecstatic that I went for 75 miles. Then Craig encouraged me to do a century, which ended up being 116 miles. Soon after that, we did two centuries, back to back. Up until that time, I had been mountain bike racing, and I hated it. But I did it to be with my husband. We definitely had different philosophies about competition. He raced to win; I raced to finish. But when he quit racing, he quit riding, and I wanted to tour. I tried to find someone to ride self-supported with me, where we'd carry our gear on the bikes, but to no avail. When I first approached Craig, he said he'd ride with me, but he wasn't carrying anything. So I settled for riding, not racing, and not carrying my stuff. By the end of that summer, I was hooked on long distances and just wanted to ride more. I'd finally found my niche.

As we went through the list, I saw the Odyssey 2000® bike ride around the world. I starred it and wrote, "In my wildest dreams," in the margin. We laughed as we compared notes, then got serious about one-week rides. We finally picked the BAK (Biking Across Kansas), but the Odyssey thing still nagged me. A couple weeks later, I sent for the information.

When my packet arrived, I started to salivate. A whole year on my bike! Three hundred sixty-six days to travel through 45 countries on six continents. The tour leaders would carry my bags, feed me and provide campsites. All I'd have to do would be ride my bike and see the world. The idea appealed to me because by that time in my career, I was burned out teaching middle-school music. I had never traveled, and there was my chance to ride, ride, ride. I mentioned it to my husband, and of course, he thought I'd lost it. Craig and I talked about it, and he decided he couldn't or didn't want to do it for several reasons. I was left to decide on my own. After many sleepless nights, I decided I could handle going alone. Once I made the decision, most of my friends accepted it as something only I would do. I had Craig's support, but my husband continued to shake his head. He just didn't understand.

After I paid my nonrefundable $500 fee in May to sign up, there was no turning back. I went to the school board in June to ask for a leave of absence because I wanted to come back to a job. In our corner of small-town rural America, we had a farmer, a housewife and a construction worker on the school board. After I asked for the leave, there was dead silence. Then the farmer asked, "Why would you want to [go]?" My reply was, "I think it would be fun." So they granted me a leave on the condition that I find someone to cover for me from January 2000 to January 2001, not a normal teaching year.

Two days after this board meeting, Craig and I left for the BAK, and I was higher than a kite. The ride across Kansas was a blast, and in the next three years we rode across Nebraska, Wisconsin, Idaho and Wyoming, telling everyone we met about the great trip I was going to take.

On the Wisconsin ride, I met a rider who was also signed up for Odyssey. We were riding up a steep hill on a rainy day and he was complaining about having cold feet. He wasn't wearing socks in an experiment to see if he could ride without them. (He didn't want to carry any around the world.) How cool. He was the only rider I met prior to arriving in Los Angeles.

Once I returned from the BAK, I turned my attention to planning. I started working three or four jobs simultaneously to make the $32,000 I needed upfront. In 1997, after 27 years of marriage, my husband and I split, and I became homeless. So in 1998, I designed and helped build my own home so I'd have someplace to come back to after Odyssey.

I was a zombie, working 16- to 18-hour days, living in a tent all summer, bathing in less than five gallons of sun-heated water in the woods, and eating only what didn't need to be cooked. I didn't know it at the time, but that summer of "roughing it" made Odyssey a piece of cake. I purposely lived in my tent and bathed elsewhere until the day my builder left. I figured if I took advantage of the shower or slept inside with the sawdust, he'd have no reason to hurry and finish.

But in late September, he did finish, four months to the day of groundbreaking, and I moved in. What a joy! I was tired. Since school started, I had been juggling my three other jobs on the side. Each day I would race home to work on the house or off to other employment. It had been months since I had slept in a bed or had more than five or six hours of sleep. I didn't know it, but that was also preparation for Odyssey.

In 1999, as each month passed, I prepared to leave my beautiful home. I found my substitute, who agreed to rent my house and drive my car. I made all financial arrangements in advance and what I couldn't finalize, I turned over to Craig. I made a will, assigned a medical power of attorney, updated my passport, and got every shot imaginable, while still working multiple jobs and riding as much as possible. By Christmas, I was ready to leave and knew everything was OK for the year. My youngest sister, Bess Robertson, did ask, "Under what circumstances would you come home?" I couldn't think of any reason because everything would be in her capable hands and those of my good friend, Craig.

The three days prior to January 1 were very unsettling for me. Suddenly, as I spent the night in Salt Lake City alone, prior to catching my plane to Los Angeles, I got scared. Did I do the right thing? I was definitely insecure. I knew very little about bike mechanics, and my big fear was getting a flat in the Rose Bowl Parade (on television). Meeting fellow riders, who seemed to be so sure of themselves, made me feel all the more shy and introverted. I was never an outgoing person, and nothing changed during those first two days of orientation. I didn't want to ask any dumb questions, so I just sat back and tried to soak it all up. I felt physically ready and just wanted to get on my bike and ride.

On the second day, we rode around the parking lot, trying to stay in straight lines. This was our preparation for the Rose Bowl Parade, the official take-off. After two hours of practice, it started to rain, and we were excused to load our bikes on the semi and pack our bags. We were finally getting close to the real thing. Though breakfast was scheduled for 4 a.m., the group was planning to party until 1 a.m. I knew I wouldn't be up that late. I was already starting the trip with a sleep deficit and was not going to add to it the first night. I can't even remember who, other than Alan, sat at the table with me for the New Year's dinner.

Those two days were a blur. I kept telling myself all through December, as I grew more tired, that I'd catch up on sleep on the trip. After all, the only thing I had to do was ride my bike and pitch my tent at night. Sounded easy to me, so I pushed myself relentlessly, preparing for school concerts, playing in the Idaho Falls Symphony and the Jackson Hole Brass Quintet, packing and repacking, making lists and checking them twice.

CHAPTER 1
Baja: Machismo

January 1 to January 18

1,098.6 miles

"If you're not living on the edge, you're taking up too much room, and I don't mean on the couch."—Bob Mack

Baja boot camp

Staff taking down portable showers

1

Baja, Mexico

The Odyssey 2000° bike trip around the world, sponsored by Tim Kneeland and Associates (TK&A), started with the Rose Bowl Parade in Pasadena. I hate to say it, but this was not what it was all cracked up to be. We had to completely strip our bikes of anything we'd added since we received it. Part of our fee for the trip included a Raleigh touring bike, manufactured to certain specifications especially for Odyssey.

I received mine November 21, 1999, the day the first real snowstorm hit Teton Valley. (Once we get this snow, it stays until spring.) We were supposed to ride this new bike, get used to it, and train on it before January 1. Let me tell you, I hated that bike. It was heavy, it had different shifters than I was used to, and the brakes made it impossible to take the front wheel off without letting all the air out of the tire. I had a bike rack that required you to take off the front tire in order to attach it. The gears were also higher than I was used to. I was in tears the few times I tried to ride it in Pocatello, Idaho, 125 miles from home and the only place close with no snow. We were told we could not change any components unless we brought spare parts with us. We were to supply our own seat and pedals, and that's all. Well, with my lack of mechanical knowledge, I wasn't about to bring anything except my front brakes. I simply could not deal with letting the air out of my tire just to be able to remove it. I went to California dreading to have to ride this bike, but wanting to ride so badly, I figured I'd adjust. And I did. By the end of the first month, I learned to love it. And I found out that I was one of the few with the original gearing on my bike, much to my dismay later on.

In the Rose Bowl Parade, we all had to wear TK&A-issued shorts, jerseys and helmets with no arm- or leg-warmers. It was in the 40s, and the wind chill, while riding, was almost unbearable. I wasn't the only one who stood around with chattering teeth. But we were tough. We had to be. We left the hotel before 5 a.m. and were on our bikes by 6:30. The parade was to start at 8 a.m., and after standing around for one and a half hours, we were chilled to the bone. By the end of the parade, my fingers wouldn't even button a button. And the worst part was we weren't even on television. Oh well. I can say I did it. We were told in the meetings that to ride again in the Rose Bowl Parade at the end of the year, we had to ride all the miles of the Odyssey trip. "OK," I said to myself, "I guess I can do that."

After the ride in front of the parade, we met up with the gear trucks, put our personalized stuff back on the bikes and dressed appropriately. Off we went down the coast of California. There had been several flat tires in the parade (they just kept pedaling) and there were several more during the day. I just kept saying my prayers. I wasn't ready to have to change a tire. Up to that point in my bike-riding experience, I had never changed a flat tire by myself. And one of my biggest fears was that I'd get left behind and get lost if I had to stop. I worried myself sick over this the first couple weeks. One poor girl had seven flats in two days.

Craig had tried to talk me into taking a class to learn a little about my bike. But I resisted because I am just not mechanically inclined and don't want to be. I just wanted to ride. He asked me several times what I'd do if I had problems out in the boonies. My reply was, "Wait until someone comes by and yell, 'Damsel in distress!'" So to this day, if I ask for any kind of help, he asks me if I'm issuing a DID call. Probably.

Our first night in camp, the two fellows next to me were reading the instructions, by flashlight, as to how to put up their tent. I still have no idea who they were, but they made me feel better about my lack of bike know-how. At least we had mechanics as staff. Prior to the trip, I had practiced putting up my tent in my living room so I knew I could crawl into it at night, and be warm and dry.

The first night's showers left a lot to be desired. I think I finally went to bed without one. TK&A had portable showers to use in campgrounds where facilities were nonexistent or insufficient. The problem was that the staff didn't yet know how to put them together. I wasn't too worried though, since I knew we had a hotel room coming up on the third day.

During the first day's ride, I met up with Sockless Bob again, a rider from Wisconsin. Sure enough, he was there in clip-on sandals. These sandals work just like biking shoes. Most riders who use them do not wear socks.

The first three days of riding were very congested, even when we crossed the border into Mexico. Thank goodness I met up with Teresa, who was able to navigate through San Diego and across the border. Being a country girl, I felt very lost in the big cities. In addition to reading the Daily Route Guide (DRG), watching street signs, and avoiding traffic and potholes, I had to dodge an airborne palm branch. I myself almost became airborne after failing to avoid a big bump in the road while gawking at something for a split second. Four-lane highways never were my favorite ride.

But on the fourth day, we finally left civilization and headed into the hills—big hills! I soon noticed men and women walking up them. I would pass these cyclists and say "Hi," and at the same time tell myself, "You are not walking for any reason." I knew I was one of the few with the original gearing, but I absolutely was not going to wimp out.

On the fifth day, a rider left the trip because he didn't like to camp. We were specifically told we'd be camping 60 percent of the time.

By the seventh day, riders were just giving up. Ninety-eight of the 244 riders left on the ride had to be sagged into camp. Eventually, riders became very creative in their sagging, thumbing rides in backs of pickups, or hiring taxis. I started labeling these weaklings as wimps. I was not going to get into camp any way other than by riding my bike. I was hurting big time though. My butt hurt, my Achilles tendons started to bother me, one day so badly I was almost in tears. But I kept riding. That's what I was there for. Plus, I was going to ride in the parade again. That was my goal!

Before I left home, I had promised Craig I'd ride a century (100 miles in one day) once a week. In exchange, he would eat just one of the Hershey's Hugs candies I'd left for him.

We had several days with mileage in the 90s, so I figured, "What's an extra five miles or so?" By the second week I was beginning to wonder if I had promised more than I could handle.

He did give me until the third week to start this promise. But the closer it got, the more impossible it seemed. It wasn't until late January that Craig responded to my many hints and sent the following email.

Date: 29 Jan 2000

Congratulations on the Century! Remember, you're TOTALLY off the hook from doing one per week. Do them just for yourself, when YOU feel like it. Be sure to take time to "smell the roses," too.

I was so grateful to have been released from what I thought was an impossible promise to keep.

Date: 29 Jan 2000

Thank you, thank you, thank you for taking me off the hook for the centuries. I am not wimpy, but I'll tell you, this is some of the hardest and most demanding riding I've ever done. Even the fast guys (and those in really good shape) were complaining by the end of this last 6 days. And Tim, the leader, just keeps pushing and telling us to ride 'til we're really tired and then 10 percent more. He didn't even ride a lot of these days when designing the route. It's a lot different driving in a car than riding it. We all know that. And I'm not sure he really realizes just how hard it has been. He did say, though, that Costa Rica and Panama should be the hardest leg of the trip. That's nice to know. So if we survived this, the rest should be a piece of cake. I'm going to hold him to that.

I was so relieved. Now I could quit obsessing over that one thing. My sister had told me several times to quit being so obsessive-compulsive, but somehow it meant more coming from Craig.

If you look at a map of Baja, Mexico, you'll notice there is really only one road from top to bottom. It was narrow, with no shoulder, and we shared it with cars, trucks, buses and whatever else needed to use it. The locals were pretty good, but the tourists were terrible. I guess they just didn't expect to see us on the road. We started out with 247 riders the first day, but by the second week, there were less than 200 cyclists on the road during any given day. Many had near misses on hills and curves. And if you did get off the road for any reason, there was no place to park your bike. Cacti and broken glass littered the roadsides. I always carried my bike to a spot where I could lay it down safely. Maybe that was why I lucked out with no flats through this section of the trip. I complained about the Baja roads a lot; but later, once we arrived in Chile, I realized the Baja roads were better than the four-lane highways we were to ride day after day.

By day 12, riding from San Ignacio to Mulege, many more people sagged from the very beginning of the day. I didn't count how many taxis went by us with bikes in them. I kept wondering why these people came on the trip. Of course, I never asked. I was still afraid to talk to them. But on that day, I started to think I wasn't as strong as I wanted to be. We had 40 kilometers of climbing with a head wind first thing in the morning, and my Achilles tendons hurt so badly I was in tears. But once Dr. Helen came along and gave me prescription-strength Naprosyn, I became my old self and completed the ride as usual.

Whew! I was worried for a while.

I was starting to get a "hard core" reputation by the end of the second week. On several occasions we camped near motels (staff were usually given rooms, which I didn't begrudge in the least). Often there would be extra rooms available that would be offered to riders by way of a drawing. My name was picked once, and I gave it back because it was a beautiful, clear night. Why would I want to pay $75 to sleep inside? I loved my tent. It was to be my home for a year. Again, I kept thinking, "Those wimps!"

For some reason, Baja seemed to be very noisy at night. I figured I'd get used to it eventually. But I certainly wasn't catching up on that sleep I needed when I left home more than two weeks before. Maybe that's why so many wanted a room with a bed. One night was particularly bad. We were camped on the lawn of a hotel in Loreto. We had our choice of the backside by the ocean (waves were too noisy) or the front side by the street (not a main drag). I picked the front because I thought the waves would keep me awake. But by 11 p.m., I had not slept a wink. I swear there are more roosters and dogs in Baja than anywhere else in the world. So when I couldn't sleep, I wrote the "Loreto Litany" on my PocketMail (a device used to send email back home).

It all starts with one barking dog that gets an urge to be vocal. Soon he has a friend who feels compelled to answer, not to be outdone by the two down the street. Now all four dogs are going at it like their vocal cords may not have a chance to work tomorrow. Not good enough. A local in-town rooster wakes up and thinks it is morning, only it is 11:45 p.m. In the background, the Friday night party animals are returning home via every imaginable motorized vehicle available. Ah, a particularly heavy-footed driver races by and yes, the dogs have gone berserk. They've picked up in intensity and have been joined by a few more. Now that I'm wide awake, I notice the heavy breathing in the tent next door, punctuated with the sneezing of another neighbor. Oh, yeah, let's hear it for the tires just squealed and the new frenzy of barking. My gosh, will there ever be peace and quiet in this small resort town? Will I ever get to sleep and rested for tomorrow's grueling 90-mile ride up and over the mountains? Are those really ocean waves I hear in the background in between all these man-made and man-caused sounds? Maybe this is a vivid dream caused by the Larium pills I started to take yesterday. That's supposed to be the main side effect. Oh, no. Now we have a zipper frenzy started. The natives are squirming in their bags. A loud radio blares past in a car. It's hopeless. Please let me awake from this bad dream.

I lay in my tent for awhile, wondering if this would go on all night. And then it got quiet. I just had to write "The Coda."

Ah, 12:40 a.m., and the dogs have ceased. The streets are almost quiet as everyone apparently made it home by the midnight curfew. Now I can hear the waves lapping on the beach. Lots of heavy breathing and the chirping of the occasional bird punctuate the night's quiet. Will it last? Will I fall into that much-awaited deep slumber that my tenting neighbors seem to be enjoying?

The next day's ride into Cuidad Constitucion, with yet another sleepless night, was hard due to lots of climbing, lots of headwind, and longer distance than the DRG said. (It was off by 20 kilometers). So that night, as I lay in my tent listening to all the noise again, I wrote "The Ciudad Constitucion Saturday Night Serenade." I was starting to count the days to La Paz, where there would be a room to block out the noise.

The serenade was written at 1:27 a.m. in hopes of becoming sleepy enough to fall asleep, no matter what.

One lone cricket keeps up his steady chirp to the loud and raucous country-and-western bass line coming from the local "bar," one block off the main street, which is the only street through town. Ah, yes, but another sleepless night. A trucker uses his jake brakes to be sure to alert all within five miles of his intent to slow down. And now the roosters are once again confused as to the time of day and begin their contest to see who can crow the longest and loudest. One high-pitched fellow can go on for a long time while "granddad" can barely get it out. It's too funny to listen to. I'm actually laughing out loud, although I'd like to put each and every one out of his misery. The cricket has not missed a beat and neither has the bass player. I can't wait for the jungle. (Joke) Oh, how I miss the peace and quiet of my home.

Day 17 had us riding into La Paz, and I was so proud of myself. We had cycled 1,232 miles since the Rose Bowl Parade with 51,400 feet of elevation gain, and I had ridden every mile. I had not taken an unprovided motel room, and I had NOT walked a single hill. I was pumped and knew I was going to be stronger for it. However, at the end of this two-and-a-half-week grueling ride, our leader, Tim, pardoned all the riders who had sagged and said they could start all over as far as riding in the parade next year. I was furious. I busted my butt, pushed myself to the limit, and now all these wimps had the same privileges as those of us who rode our hearts out. I felt betrayed. I didn't dislike any of the riders because I realized we weren't all made from the same mold, and many of them were becoming my friends, but it was the principle of the matter. Why tell us one thing and then do another? Not only that, we had listened to Tim rant and lecture us about sagging since the beginning. I knew I'd get over feeling betrayed. I was stronger for persevering and more determined than ever to ride every mile.

Up to this point, the ride was referred to as "boot camp," subjecting us to marginal camping facilities with no grass, water hauled in and purified, beans and rice for days on end, bad roads, lots of hills, sleepless nights due to an exorbitant number of roosters and dogs, and relentless lectures about our lack of preparation for the trip. I loved every minute despite the hardships and had only one 10-second thought that "Teaching school would have been easier than this."

CHAPTER 2
Costa Rica and Panama: Sick and Stubborn

January 18 to January 31

1,524.0 miles to date

"The 'Spirit Force' behind you is greater than the task before you." —Linda Cook

Al at a Costa Rican bus stop the day after climbing the Mountain of Death

Al on the crest of the Mountain of Death, Costa Rica

2

Costa Rica and Panama

A flight out of La Paz took us into San Jose, Costa Rica. We had had a long day, getting up at 4:30 a.m. and riding our bikes to the airport. We had to prepare our own bikes for the plane by removing pedals, pumps, bags and cyclometers; turning the handlebars; and letting air out of our tires. This was to be the routine every time we flew. Due to miscalculations of cargo space, we ended up taking two planes instead of one.

It was dark by the time our second plane landed, so we were bused to our hotel that was to be home for the next three nights. I spent two days resting and touring the area. In Costa Rica, the hills were definitely mountains. Many big volcanoes appeared when the clouds lifted, so we knew there'd be lots more climbing.

Our first day out of Santiago was a killer. It turned out to be 150 kilometers, 80 of which were uphill with no break, and 46 were downhill with no break. The other 25 were up and down. It is really hard to ride up, up, up with no chance to rest the quads and calves, and just as hard to go down, seemingly forever, with no chance to rest your hands (which are on the brakes). I'd much rather have up and down with variety along the way.

We started to climb immediately upon leaving the hotel and soon encountered a headwind to boot. The higher we climbed, the colder and wetter it got. We actually rode through a cloud forest, which is a fine mist, but after a long time, you get wet. The fog was so thick that visibility became almost nonexistent. And then the cloud forest turned into a RAIN forest. We had been advised to take extra clothes for the cool downhill ride, which I did, so I was carrying extra weight uphill for a long time. I wanted to save those clothes until the top so I could start down warm and dry. I only stopped long enough to grab a Power Bar or cookies, but every time I stopped, I got colder and colder. At one point, when the roads were wet, trucks kept going by, and the fog was dangerously thick, I thought about sagging in. I had lost count of the numerous pickups that had gone by with bikes in them. Taxis had been busy ever since we first left town. I even saw two semitrucks go by with bikes strapped on their cargo.

By checkpoint (where we would sign in at midday), it was 2:30 p.m. and rather late since I still had many miles to go. I was starting to feel defeated. So many miles to go and daylight was running out. I wanted to do this ride, but I was feeling skeptical. By the time I reached the next-to-the-last summit, I was chilled to the bone, my food was almost gone, and no one was continuing to ride on. Dozens of riders were staying put at a summit restaurant until they could catch a ride. I found out later that one cyclist and his bike rode in the back of a pickup with only a wooden pallet-type divider between him and a bull. Others had paid a farmer to ride in the back of his big farm truck right along with the manure. People were desperate. Luckily, I found Inge, a strong German lady, who was willing to continue the ride with me. We changed into our driest clothes and bundled up the best we could for the final 11-kilometer ascent to the 11,171-foot summit of the Mountain of Death—its name, literally.

By the time Inge and I reached San Ysidro at the bottom of that 46-kilometer downhill (I didn't know there was anyplace in the world where you could ride downhill for so long), it was 6 p.m. and dark. We still had several miles to go since camp was on the other side of town. We hung really close to each other, using streetlights and car lights to navigate. We finally gave up and walked the last five blocks because it was just too dangerous to ride. But WE MADE IT. It was 6:30 and only 73 riders had made it all the way. People were still arriving by their sag vehicle of choice at 10 p.m. that night. I was exhausted, but elated to know I could do that tough ride when so many others couldn't or wouldn't. None of the people I had started with finished that day.

It was hard to get up the next morning, but the ride started out much easier. Gentle ups and downs. Now this was my style of riding—but it didn't last. Right after midday checkpoint, we turned onto a secondary road and went up another volcano—straight up. I was just as wet that day from the heat and humidity as I was the day before from the cold and rain. What a drastic change! Our bodies had to adapt so quickly from one extreme to the next. The grade was the steepest I had ever seen. In Costa Rica, they don't contour around any hill; they go straight up the ridgeline. I was able to stay on my bike as I passed numerous others walking again. I *was* getting stronger. The highlight of the day was when I rode past four guys and two girls who were walking, and I was older than all of them. Many cyclists were intimidated by the steepness and once again, many became creative in their sagging. None of my buddies made it that day either. I seemed to be riding by myself a lot. I was too slow to keep up with the really macho crowd and too stubborn to quit when my buddies did.

As I neared my goal of San Vito, it just had to rain again on the steep descent into town. Hairpin turns on slick roads are not my idea of a good time. But we had to ride what was in front of us. A couple riders did fall on the last descent; just lots of road rash and hurt egos. We were blessed with pizza for dinner at a local restaurant, but camping facilities ranked right up there with the worst. Water was standing on the athletic field where we were to camp, so many of us crowded inside on the concrete floor of the athletic building. We still pitched our tents inside the building, and that left inches between us. The bathroom facilities were less than acceptable. This was the night things took a real turn for the worse. We were all exhausted after two grueling days of riding, and now we had to deal with cold, wet, and/or hard-floor camping conditions. Sanitation was an issue and on top of all this, I started feeling really sick to my stomach about two hours after dinner. I lay awake all night while that pizza did flipflops.

The next morning I was sicker than ever and signed up for a TK&A sag. After breakfast I told myself to get a grip and ride. The first 30 kilometers were more of the steepest riding we had done so far, and I had to get off and walk twice. I was bummed, but I just couldn't push that hard the way I felt. At the top was a reward: the most beautiful sight we'd seen, with lush green growth everywhere. And the ride down was even better, with gorgeous views and birds singing on that sunny, warm day. Once we hit the level bottom, it became very hot and humid, and I felt sicker and sicker. After a laborious two-and-a-half-hour border crossing, I had to take my first sag, sharing a taxi with Susan. I was sick from the heat and exhaustion, and even sicker that I had become a wimp. I wanted to cry! I had done the most strenuous riding of the day and could not push on. My body was shutting down.

It was really hot in David, Panama, and we were to camp in a gym with no air movement. I decided since I was a wimp that day that I might as well get an air-conditioned room and try to get some sleep, which I did. I felt much better the next morning until the stench of rotting road kill about knocked me off my bike. I was an early riser and on the road between 6:30 and 7 a.m. every day to beat the heat, but by 8 a.m., it was sweltering again. There are only so many clothes you can take off. I wondered how people lived in those conditions day after day. I'd much rather live in a cold climate and have to add layers. By midafternoon, the heat was really getting to me again. The temperature registered 104 degrees (and that was probably in the shade). Hot blasts would come out of the woods and feel like a furnace. After experiencing chills and the shakes, I decided to rest in the shade for a while and then, later, pushed on, only to have to get off my bike down the road again. I finally sagged in with Mark and Sandy in the back of a pickup. I had become a true wimp, and I hated myself. As we rode into camp, two of my biking buddies, Tom and Dick, applauded as they saw me exit the pickup. I immediately got lectured about being so hard on myself. I decided tomorrow would be another day.

That night ranked as another of the worst campsites. It was along a river in which you could bathe, had lots of bugs, and had only a hole in the ground for a bathroom. (Portable toilets were brought in much later.) It also rated the worst meal of the trip. As I walked through the dinner line, there was nothing but fruit this and fruit that. I can't eat fruit when I feel good and for sure not when I'm sick. There was nothing with any substance from which to pick. I couldn't even eat. I just lay in my tent and felt sorry for myself. All my dreams shattered because I couldn't handle the heat. I was sick all night, alternating with the sweats and the chills, and the next morning I had to sag with TK&A. I was so weak I could hardly walk from my tent to breakfast, which was awful again. All I can remember are soupy eggs and more fruit. How did they expect us to ride on less-than-sufficient food?

My first day as a sagger with TK&A was the pits. It took us six hours to go 85 miles because we'd go as far as checkpoint and then sit for hours. I vowed never to do that again. I just had to stay healthy. Next day was the ride into Panama City over the canal. I rode and felt like myself again. So good to be back on the bike and even better to be done with that hot humid stretch. I was looking forward to moving on.

Probably one of the hardest things I've ever had to do in my lifetime is deal with my inadequacies. As a child, I could never measure up to my dad's expectations, no matter how hard I tried. And I tried hard. My dad wanted me to get all A's in school, and if I got one B, he focused on the B, not all the other A's. I always took care of the family garden while living at home. And I was proud of how neat it looked. I was so proud one time that I had my dad come out and look at it, and I had missed one weed. It was right in the pea row and blended in perfectly. What did he see? Not the clean rows but the one weed I had missed.

Then I went off to college, and once again, I was better than average, but not really good musically compared to some others. I always felt second-best. Never first chair or lead in a production. Just average.

I got married and was so excited to be accepted for what I was. At least I thought I was. I soon found out that my husband expected more and more from me athletically than I ever dreamed myself capable of doing. I had never participated in sports in school and wasn't what you'd call physically fit. But I had enthusiasm and was willing to try almost anything because as a kid, I did nothing. So I got into mountain climbing, biking, and cross-country and alpine skiing. I was in heaven doing all these new things, and doing them quite well considering I didn't learn until I was in my 20s. But as time progressed, I was pressured to push harder and try to keep up. No matter how hard I tried, I could never catch up because my husband just got better, too. It was frustrating to push, push, push and feel like I was losing ground.

Then my husband took up mountain bike racing and cross-country ski racing. I resisted, but after a year, I decided to try it just so I could be with him and share the experience. He raced to win; I raced to finish. I didn't really care if I came in last. Not good enough. It was like I could never do my own thing; I was always expected to meet someone else's goals. I was so glad when we quit racing. I then took up my own style of biking, touring at my own pace. All throughout my married life, I could never reach the goals set for me by my husband. It was a very frustrating time.

I've always set high goals for myself, often in addition to those set for me by others. So when I started Odyssey, my main goal was to ride every mile, every day. Imagine my frustration the first time that didn't happen. I almost felt like I was being punished for something, when in reality, I was human and fragile like everyone else. I expected more out of my body. Never mind that I was 52 years old and past my prime. I soon had to realize that I wasn't capable of keeping up with the younger ones and that germs would invade my body no matter how diligent I was in my personal hygiene. Panama was the beginning of having to slow down and take even better care of myself. I wasn't a wimp, but I saw my inability to reach my goal as a weakness that I did not want to accept.

CHAPTER 3
Chile:
Confusion, Guilt Trip
and Change of Heart

January 31 to February 15

2,279.4 miles to date

"This, too, shall pass."—Bess Robertson, my sister

Al frustrated with rainy conditions in Chile

Al with a phone in the middle of nowhere

3

CHILE

Our flight from Panama City to Santiago, Chile, was anything but smooth. We had a 16-hour delay from the outset due to mechanical problems with the plane. Now, I never liked to fly, and when I considered this trip, the one thing that made me think twice was the number of flights. I've always been rather squeamish at take-off and landing, but I decided to get over it. But when our departure kept getting delayed, I became a "Nervous Nellie" again. And then to top it off, 75 bikes and some other gear had to be left behind because of a weight constraint. They were to travel on another plane later. I kept wondering if they really left out enough weight. Was this flight really safe? Ah, the stress of it all. We did arrive in Santiago safely, but the left-behind gear didn't arrive until two days later. So we ended up with two extra layover days.

While we were in Santiago waiting for the rest of our gear, we heard of an Alaskan Airlines plane crash. I immediately wrote to Craig and my youngest sister, Bess, to let them know how important they both were to me and explained my fear of flying in depth to them. I really didn't want to hear about plane problems.

Date: 2 Feb 2000
To: Craig and Bess
Subject: Plane crash

Big news here today is, of course, the Alaskan Airlines crash. We have a biker who left his job as a pilot for that airline to do Odyssey and one of our staff people is a former Alaskan

Airlines employee. The biker-pilot knew the pilot and the staff person had several former friend-employees on that flight. And that same staff person confided in me today that she was scared for the first time the other night when we flew after such a long delay. Glad she didn't tell me that night. I was scared enough already. That's not the way I want to go.

Please don't alarm Mom and Dad, or any other family or friends. This is a confidential baring of the soul, but I really don't feel safe with our flight arrangements so far. And, of course, a water crash would be the world's worst (for me). I've always had a fear of drowning ever since my pool accident when I was in junior high. You know some childhood memories scar you for life. But, I will be strong and say my prayers and hopefully my time won't be up while on an airplane. Just know that I'm more afraid of that than any big city street. We were warned here to be very careful and even so, one of our cyclists had all his money taken out of his front short's pocket. Next time I go out in these big cities, the pepper mace is going with me. Just let them try anything. One never knows about this cruel world. I've seen lots of tragic deaths the past couple years, and it really makes one realize just how fragile we all are. Please know that you are the two most cherished people in my world, and you are in my thoughts daily.

After spending three days in Santiago, we finally got to ride. The swollen ankles I'd had for two days were better, but I had a rash on one leg that morning. That was just one more irritation. Two days later when the rash became painful and spread over my knee, it was diagnosed as shingles. Now I really needed that.

From what I gather, shingles are the manifestation of a chicken pox virus that lies dormant in the body and is reactivated under stress. There was nothing to do except let it run its course and try not to scratch.

We were riding the four-lane Highway 5, due south. I was thinking, "Aren't there any roads other than four-lane, interstate-like roads on which to ride?" I finally had my first flat tire due to glass on those shoulders, but friendly and mechanically inclined Barb happened along and helped me. I knew I wasn't going to get lost on that big highway, so it didn't bother me too much. It was more of an inconvenience than anything else. I was just glad I'd made it that long before getting a flat. On my birthday, I got a wake-up call from Beth. At the water station where we filled our water bottles, fellow riders sang "Happy Birthday" to me. This was the day we got off the four-lane highway and onto more friendly backroads. Yeah! At midday checkpoint, the riders there sang to me again, and Chuck recited the following poem by H.S. Fritsch.

How Old Are You?

Age is the quality of mind,
If you've left your dreams behind,
If hope is cold,
If you no longer look ahead,

If ambition's fires are dead,
Then you are old.
But if from life you take the best,
If in life you keep the jest,
If love you hold,
Then no matter how the years go by,
No matter how the birthdays fly,
You are not old.

I was flattered. This was very appropriate for me. I had begun to get to know a few people on the trip, and they made my day. Soon after checkpoint, Beth got a flat and I was able to help her change it. This was very fulfilling for me.

I had made previous arrangements with Craig to call him on my birthday, one of three phone calls I had planned to make during the course of the year. But for an hour or two on either side of the agreed upon time, we were in the boonies with no phones available. I made the comment to Beth, jokingly, about how nice it would be if a phone just appeared for me. About 20 minutes later, there was a phone on a fence post with nothing else around for miles. But, alas, it did not work. I had been having problems with phones in Chile. All my email was transmitted by phone with a Sharp TM-20 PocketMail device. I was using a calling card supplied by my friend, Mary, but this calling card didn't work on all phones. I needed a CTC or Entel phone, and this was a GTV. But the thought was nice. I was able to find a phone that worked that evening after walking the streets for quite a while, and I did get to talk to Craig. It was so good to hear his voice.

The weather was much more bearable in Chile until the third day, when we got rain. Two days later, it became quite steady and irritating. When you ride through four inches of water and can't see what's in the bottom of the muddy puddles, it is disconcerting, to be sure. On the way into the Villarrica camp, we rode a very narrow two-lane road with gravel washed onto the edges in places. This caused us to have to weave into the traffic lane more often than we wanted to. I almost lost it once when my rear wheel didn't follow me. I wrenched my arm trying to stay upright, which I did, but that was one more pain I didn't need. About this time, the shingles decided to spread to my back, and it was becoming even more difficult to sleep at night. Along with the extreme crotch pain I'd had for the last four weeks, I was becoming a little irritable.

I did receive encouraging emails from one Webpage reader, and that really made my day.

Date: 7 Feb 2000
From: Noreen

Hi, Al! Hope you have some relief with your new Terry saddle. Too bad about the shingles. Remember "that which doesn't kill us, makes us stronger." Right? I love that you're riding every day because you "signed up for a bike ride!" I'm sure I'm only one of many other women who wish they could be riding with you. Take care of yourself and have fun!

Date: 12 Feb 2000
From: Noreen
Subject: Moral support

Al, listen to your body! When you need a day off, take it. Don't worry about keeping your vow to "ride every mile." Just enjoy your adventure and have a great time. I'm so sorry to hear about the shingles. I hope you are relieved of that irritation soon. I'm thoroughly enjoying your journal. Thanks for sharing the ups and downs (both literally and figuratively) with the rest of us. Take care and best wishes.

I also wrote to Bess asking for advice. I wanted to be sure I was doing the right thing.

Date: 10 Feb 2000
Subject: Shingles

Boy do these things get ugly. I have not scratched any of them; they don't itch, but they turn a dark ugly red. I look like I have the plague. There are four stages on my right knee area and now I have new ones all over my back. There is nerve pain in the right groin area but no bumps there. Is this weird or what? Hasn't kept me from riding yet. They are just UGLY. I notice them most at night, when they cause a burning or tingling sensation. And I've been waking up, twice last night, absolutely drenched in sweat. Is this normal? I was so wet last night that I needed to dry off with a towel. My clothes were soaked and it wasn't because it was hot outside my tent. Quite the contrary. What is wrong with me? I am supposed to be the epitome of good health.

I'd hate to be a sicky on this trip. I know several cyclists who have had the coughing crud since the first week in Mexico. Glad I don't have that. I take my vitamin C every day and am trying to get decent sleep every night. I just want to be normal again. OK, I'm asking for nurse input here.

So when I woke up the next morning in Villarrica to more heavy rain, I decided to take a taxi with Alice and Cheryl to the next town, Valdivia. It rained hard all day and with everything that hurt, I was in no mood to battle the elements and fight for my space on what had become very narrow, sometimes shoulderless secondary roads. I just didn't feel safe in those riding conditions. Boy, had I turned into a wimp or what.

Our camp that night was a field of mud. Thankfully our organizer was able to get a college gymnasium for the night, but no tents. So we slept body to body on the gym floor while our wet tents grew mold and bacteria in their stuff sacks. I was so glad to be inside though. The rain and wind were incessant all night long. It sounded like the roof would lift and take off several times. I got no sleep whatsoever. I lay there and made myself physically sick listening to the storm and thinking about the next day. How could I ride in weather like that? Should I risk my life on the road? More wimp feelings. The really hard-core riders were still riding every day, even though they were becoming fewer in number as the days passed. On many days, less than 100 cyclists chose to ride. And it was never the same 100. Everyone, including me, seemed to be trying to find themselves. I was disgusted that I had let all these adversities affect me this way, but on the other hand, I felt like, "If it isn't any fun, why should I be doing it?"

We looked outside that next morning and the rain was going sideways. That's how hard the wind was blowing. When many of the dedicated and experienced riders bagged it on that day out of Valdivia, I felt better about myself. Then two of my "sagger buddies" accused me of becoming one of them. I wanted to ride, but I wanted to be safe. I didn't want to be a wimp, but I wanted to live. Why was I having such a hard time? Was it because I was tired, scared or just expecting too much of myself? I had hit a wall. I just couldn't keep pushing, and I hated myself.

I sent an email to Craig so he'd know how I felt. He was my sounding board.

Date: 10 Feb 2000

Hope I get out of this slump soon. I'm really tired and don't have the guts to push in this weather. Maybe I set my goals too high for myself. That's a bummer. I'm still having a good time and am really glad I'm here. Just not willing to risk my life yet.

I rode the next day and, yes, we had rain, but it was so beautiful and the roads were better. Camp that night was a low swampy area along a river. The only decent spots to pitch a tent were on hillsides. Very few people camped, and I almost envied those who found rooms because it was bad. But I wasn't ready to wimp out and pay for a room. I was still out for an adventure, and as long as I didn't roll out my door, I'd be OK.

The next morning it was still raining, but we were to traverse the Andes and I was riding no matter what. From Entre Lagos, where we camped, to the summit was beautiful but rainy. Cliff bands with waterfalls became prominent and the vegetation was lush. Should be, it rains there constantly. The awesome scenery kept my mind off how cold and wet I was getting.

By the time I got to the summit, it was snowing big wet flakes, and I was cold and wanted to change into my warmer and dry clothes. Only there was nowhere to change. I went behind a sign and stripped down to my underwear and changed my clothes there. I didn't care. You have to do what you have to do to survive sometimes.

Unfortunately the nice highway turned to a gravel road, more suitable for mountain biking. Imagine a road under construction. We rode touring bikes over basic gravel with lots of potholes, some big rocks not totally covered, ruts where the gravel was soft, narrow sections and fist-size rocks that were prominent now and then. Thank goodness I had mountain biking experience. One of my friends, Cheryl, hadn't, and she had stopped, and was crying and shaking. I felt sorry for her. I walked with her for awhile and then gave her a couple hugs and went on my way. Eventually, she was able to catch a sag.

Once we hit the border, I figured the road would improve, but it only deteriorated. The gravel gave way to slimey goo. Cars would whip by me and my bike, coating us both with brown muck. I don't know who I felt sorrier for, my bike or myself. I did find a hose in camp, in Villa La Angostura, and cleaned my bike first thing upon arrival. I was glad to have left Chile and was hoping that our ride in Argentina would be better. It was. We woke up to 32 degrees and ice crystals on our tents, but the sun was out, and we passed freshly snow-covered peaks on the glorious ride into

Bariloche. The scenery reminded me of home, and I felt rejuvenated. I was going to be OK; I just knew it.

Camp in Bariloche was a horse pasture, and the flies were bad. But at least it wasn't raining. I could handle it. And those who found accommodations in town missed out on the highlight of the camp, a seat attached to a cable that went downhill rather quickly. What a gas! I dragged the chair up the hill twice and rode down. It just seemed to let all those past frustrations loose. I felt like a kid, whooping and hollering. Riders were still lugging the seat up the hill just before dark. Perfect ending to a stressful two weeks.

It was rather disconcerting, at least to me, to be so sure of myself and then become not so sure of myself. When you think you have all "your ducks in a row" and then find out you don't, you become confused and incapable of making solid decisions. Once I got sick and realized I couldn't ride every mile every day, I got depressed. All of a sudden I started feeling guilty about some of the decisions I was starting to make. Am I being wimpy? Will people think I'm turning into a coward? Should I push a little harder? What if I fall apart? All these questions and no answers. I wanted to take a day off, but I wanted to ride. I made myself physically sick worrying about whether I should ride in certain conditions or not. I was becoming a nervous wreck because I felt guilty every time I didn't ride. But yet I didn't want to put myself in danger.

I received two emails that turned me around. One was from a fellow biker friend telling me to play more and that everyone back home knew I could do it, so I didn't need to prove anything to anyone. He actually told me to get off my guilt trip. The other one was from someone reading my Webpage, commending me for making safe decisions.

Date: 12 Feb 2000
From: Bill via Craig

I would like to get a message to Al to give her some encouragement on her trip. An effective cyclist is one who can use a bicycle with confidence and competence for pleasure, for utility, or for sport under all highway conditions and conditions of climate, terrain, and traffic. An effective cyclist knows when conditions become too dangerous and packs it in. Al is an effective cyclist and not "one of them!" I enjoy reading Al's journal every day, and since I have traveled First-, Second-, and Third-World countries, I can relate to her stories. I wanted to do this ride, but my job would not allow it. Maybe next time. Al, ride safely and keep writing those stories.

Both of these confirmed my feelings that maybe I shouldn't ride all the time. No one wrote and said, "ride, ride, ride." So I had a heart-to-heart talk with myself and said, "Get a life and stop worrying so much." That was when I made the decision to go off-route (sign off the bike ride and do something else for a day or two) when something interesting came along, and if conditions, weather-wise or health-wise, were marginal, I sagged. My body reacted favorably, and I started seeing more of the sights. But oh, the trauma I went through to come to that decision.

The one thing I learned by that point on the trip was that no one expected more out of me than myself.

CHAPTER 4
Africa:
Fear and the Unknown

February 15 to March 16

3,649.8 miles to date

*"It is not really an adventure unless at some point you ask,
'What the **** am I doing here?'"—Dick Ryan*

Willma in the boonies of Africa

Nancy and Arnie with one of many flat tires

4

Africa

We left Bariloche, Argentina, for Africa via a 747 stretch plane, owned and piloted by the Prince of Qatar. The runway at Bariloche is not used for planes of that size. Our pilot purposely only took on only enough fuel to get us to Buenos Aires so he'd have less weight to lift off the short runway. We had been instructed to get our bags down to 60 pounds per person, and I know that was hard because some of our gear was still wet from the past few days. I was sure hoping everyone tried to reach the allotted weight. The most disconcerting moment was when he backed up to the very edge of the runway to give us every available inch for take-off. Rider/ex-pilot Erik said loudly, "We'll be lucky if we get off the ground." Not what I wanted to hear! I was holding my breath, and as we lifted off at the last second, a roaring cheer from the more than 200 cyclists erupted. More stress.

A few hours before landing in Johannesburg, South Africa, a copy of the following email circulated amongst the cyclists. A rider had received it from a friend back home who felt compelled to pass the information along.

I have with me three folks from South Africa with some pertinent hints for safe passage while in S.A. I'm not trying to be an alarmist, but forewarned is forearmed, and this is very practical information direct from locals.

1. Never cycle or travel alone or in small groups. A good minimum would be 12, and six should be males.

2. Rape is an enormous problem in S.A. The myth among the locals is that the HIV virus can be eliminated by sexual contact with AIDS-free persons. Therefore, fresh, foreign females are fair game. It's a male-dominated society, and women are fair game in terms of culture. There is a lot of anger left over from the apartheid, hence women bear the brunt of much of it.
3. Never leave your bike unattended. Keep your passport and wallet on you at all times. When getting cash from ATMs, make sure you are not being watched. Do not count bills in public.
4. This may not apply to S.A., but make inquiries about renewed outbreaks of tsetse flies that cause fatal sleeping sickness. There is no cure or preventive medicine at this time.
5. Never bathe in rivers, and never drink or shower in untreated water because of bilharzia and flukes. Sanitation is poor in most rural areas. Regard all water as suspect.
6. Especially in northern S.A., take your malaria prevention seriously.
7. Concerning point 2, insist on more than one checkpoint daily. The distances you are traveling in the heat of summer are vast for this part of the world. Stragglers and small groups may be robbed or attacked. You must account for everyone, all day!
8. Generally the cities and built-up areas will be safer than rural areas. Without some kind of security present, my three friends would not attempt to navigate your intended route.
9. Having said all the above, you will meet wonderful people, see gorgeous scenery and have an extraordinary experience.

I was wondering why our tour leader would take us to such a place. I had never felt comfortable in unfamiliar surroundings, and it had always been hard for me to talk to people I didn't know. I classified myself as an introvert, although as early as March, some of my new friends laughed at that. I would usually stand back while others took over. That's why I hardly talked to a soul the first two days of orientation. However, once I felt comfortable, there was no holding back. I had always shied away from new foods or wearing new styles of clothes. "Just not me," I'd say. I had this great fear of the unknown. So why did I come on this trip? I told myself it was to ride my bike and have an adventure. I was hoping to get over some of my insecurities, but after reading the email, I wasn't sure.

I never mentioned that email to my family until after we left Africa, and I tried not to worry too much when I first read it, but it certainly was in the back of my mind for the next month.

In Johannesburg, our tour leader, Tim, did tell us not to ride alone anymore. So on the first day five of us formed a group. We had Beth, a nurse, who became our leader, and I was co-pilot. It was often necessary to have two or more people reading the Daily Route Guide (DRG) since they could be quite confusing. Rip was our blessed mechanic. Not only did he help us change flat tires, he also helped others along the way. Dick was the humorist and kept us in stitches with his quotes for the day, and Tom was a geologist for which I was very grateful. I had always had an interest in geology and asked a hundred questions about what we were seeing. It seemed the mountains were always changing, and I was fascinated with their beauty. We named ourselves the "Young at Heart" group even though our accumulative ages totaled more than 250.

We stopped at a gas station early that first morning to use the facilities and asked about the safety of riding alone. The locals confirmed our worst fears. "Never walk or ride alone in Africa." OK. I had taken every other warning we were given pretty seriously, so I wasn't about to test the waters here.

A couple days after Johannesburg, I wrote to Craig explaining my fears. I was trying to give him some insight on my mental and physical state and he replied with the following email.

Date: 20 Feb 2000
Subject: Photos, morale, gripes, Oh my!

Time to take a deep breath…inhale…exhale…There. Don't you feel better? No? OK, lock yourself in the bathroom, and scream at the top of your lungs. Better now? Good!

Do you recall before you left on this trip, I predicted that about six weeks into the year would be a real low point for your (and everyone's) attitudes? Well, guess where you are…six weeks (OK, it's seven weeks, but that's still pretty close). The honeymoon period is over. People are getting a little tired, physically, mentally, and of each other.

I also predicted that you'd survive this low point, and the strong ones (especially you) would grow out of it, as the true characters develop. Pushing through this is what separates the "men from the boys."

Time for another deep breath? Or a loud scream? Go ahead…you've earned it.

Concentrate on preserving and enhancing your "mental and physical state." This is YOUR vacation. So make it your vacation. Do what you want (and need) to do. If you don't feel like riding, then don't. If you do, then do. And feel free to change your mind as time progresses. It doesn't matter if you thought (and maybe said) you wanted to do something a particular way. If you now think otherwise, go for it.

Wow, what a friend. Not only did he take care of things back home for me, but he also helped me stay on track when things got tough. I thought I had already let him down when I backed out of the century promise. I just wanted to do what I said I'd do.

I knew we were heading toward Kruger Park where heavy rain had reportedly damaged roads. We were told in Middelburg that the roads past the next day's scheduled campsite no longer existed due to extreme flooding. I was worried more about sanitation than anything since outhouses were very prominent in the country as well as in the shantytowns on the outskirts of cities. We could smell the raw sewage while riding along the roads. I didn't eat anything that wasn't cooked, so this limited my diet somewhat. I did eat a lot of prepackaged foods like cookies, Power Bars, and candy bars. And I was lucky in that I did not suffer the gastrointestinal disorders that lots of other riders had for days on end. I only had one quick bout one morning. Some riders were always sick. It had started in Baja, Mexico, and for some, it was still with them two months later in South Africa. We had been warned about fresh vegetables and fruit way back in Chile because produce was often irrigated with sewage water. So I just didn't take any chances. As it turned out, we only had one detour because a bridge was out. We were traveling right on the edge of the heavy rain area.

After crossing into Swaziland, we needed to use the restrooms. They were so smelly and gross that two of us girls went out behind the building and used a bush, all the while thinking, "Just how bad would it be to get caught?" That wasn't the only time we did this during the trip.

As we entered Swaziland, we encountered road construction going up a particularly long hill. The shoulder was covered with slippery red mud that made for less than optimum riding conditions. About half way up that hill, a car passed carrying six young men who jeered at me. They were definitely NOT friendly, and my riding buddy, Inge, was up the hill several hundred feet in front of me. I felt very vulnerable and quite scared for a while, even though the car kept going. I was never threatened physically, but that incident unnerved me.

When we finally reached the top, the sky opened up and we became drenched in a matter of seconds. As we slowly went down the other side, we came upon Organist Bill and Margherita, two really good, strong riders, who had had an accident trying to avoid a fast approaching car. That did it. I was off my bike and walking. I could not force myself to ride in those conditions. Clearly the wet roads had been the cause of their accident. No one was hurt badly, unless you consider ugly road rash bad, but the potential for serious injuries was there.

So I sagged my scared body into our Mbabane, Swaziland, camp where I was greeted with a very soggy campground. There was absolutely no dry spot to be found. I just pitched my tent on what looked like the least flooded area and resigned myself to being wet for the night. Dinner, which looked really unappetizing, was served on paper plates and there was no place to sit. We had to stand outside in the rain. Only time in my life I ever ate with rain puddles on my plate. I went to bed thinking, "I can't take much more of this wet weather." There's a reason why I don't live in the Seattle area.

When I awoke in the morning, it was still raining, and I wrestled with myself over riding in unsafe conditions or catching a bus ahead to Durban with about 70 other riders. Another hard decision, but it became easy once we heard about another rider, Bobbi, being hit by a car on the wet roads soon after she had left camp that morning. I was out of there and not on my bike. I paid my $30 to ride a bus to Durban and shared a hotel room with Dick and Tom for the next three days while the rest of the cyclists rode and caught up to us.

While in Durban, I rested, did chores, and got used to city life. We had to watch our backs for the ever-present muggers. Parents would use their children to distract people while they picked pockets ever so expertly. After spending four days in Durban, I sent the following email back home to Craig and Bess.

Date: 28 Feb 2000
Subject: Incidents

I'm sending this info because I think you should be aware of it although be careful who you tell (such as Mom and Dad and not the Web). I've had no problems myself and am being very careful, but anything could happen.

Two male riders were walking home late one evening on a side street (DUH) and were accosted. Knives were pulled, but they were able to get away unharmed.

Two other riders had their money picked out of their pockets while walking on a busy street during the day. This could happen in any big city (so I told myself).

Tim and Ann had arranged to have a van delivered to wherever they were along with another van for some other riders. On the way to them, one of the vans was hijacked and shots were fired at the van when the driver tried to avoid having the van taken. Finally he gave up and got another van. (Why on earth Tim and Ann wanted another van after that, I don't know.)

Tom and Dick were walking from the Holiday Inn, where we stayed while in Durban, to the City Lodge where our layover accommodations were for the weekend. Two blocks from the City Lodge, a robbery had just taken place and while the robbers were fleeing down the alley, gunfire was exchanged. Tom and Dick were five feet from the entrance of that alley on the other side of the street and were very close to being in the line of fire.

Al and Steve (Stephanie), husband and wife, were walking down a major street sidewalk in broad daylight and were attacked by five young men. Both were thrown to the ground but rescued by locals when they screamed for help. The muggers didn't get anything, and they are OK.

All these incidents happened in three days and in a big city. That's one reason I hate coming into the big cities. And every time we have a layover day, it's in a blasted big city. What's the fascination? I try to stay off the street and go out with street-wise people when I have to be out. I much prefer the remote countryside. Maybe I'll change my mind after the next three days, but we'll see. This is supposed to be the most dangerous area according to some people. I will be careful.

Most of these people have opted to not ride these next few days. I understand their fear, even though I think you have to look at the big city versus the remoteness, and I'm not sure there is a direct correlation. I could be wrong. I know how I felt (frightened and very uneasy) when I was jeered at by the carload of males while climbing a steep hill by myself, so I can't knock their decision to not ride. Some were visibly shaken by their experience, and none of them are young and inexperienced.

We left Durban and headed for the Transkei region, a previously politically volatile area. Some riders did "research" and found out that we should not go into that area. I kept thinking, "Why are we here if it's that bad?" Of course, many locals still harbored ill feelings, and they made it sound worse than it really was. But how were we to know? I just thought, "Well, the sun is shining, and I can take a lot more when it is," so I decided to go on with the cyclists. I remember saying, "I guess if your time is up, it doesn't really matter where you are." Safety was supposed to be a big issue with TK&A, so I had to trust. There was another busload of riders who defected, some of the same cyclists who had come to Durban early, plus a few others. Never in Africa did the entire group ride on any one day.

South Africa was beautiful country—with long rolling hills that seemed to go on forever, ever-changing mountainous topography and animals uncommon to most of us, including giraffes, baboons, monkeys and elephants. It was a shame we couldn't relax and enjoy it. One group of ladies, Dr. Helen, Mechanic Barb, Dr. Charmaine and Linda, rented their own van to use as a personal sag wagon and even had a sign made that said "Women's Undercover Sag" with their own logo. That was their way of dealing with the safety issues.

The Transkei region was geologically the most beautiful we'd seen. What struck me were the green, lush rolling hillsides and river gorges, with some jagged peaks in the background. However, once again, fear took over. When my riding buddies, Ed and Willma, decided to sag at checkpoint one day, I found another rider, Dean, to accompany me. Soon after checkpoint, we entered a small town on the way to Umtata. We were the only white people in the entire town, we were on bikes, and the streets were crawling with thousands of people. The town just happened to be built on a long slope, so our riding speed slowed considerably. I was OK until this fellow pushing a wheel barrel started walking alongside me yelling in his native tongue. He didn't look particularly friendly, but I couldn't tell. I just tried to go faster. He went faster. I pushed a little harder and he started to run alongside me, still yelling. I gave it everything I had, and he set his wheel barrel down and started running beside me, flailing his arms wildly and yelling at the top of his lungs. I was petrified. I was sure he didn't like me for some reason and that his next move would be to attack me. Dean was right behind me, but I knew there was nothing he could do if this guy let loose. I just kept pushing even as my legs and lungs were burning. We finally reached the crest of the hill and escaped. Dean admitted he was a little uneasy, too.

Right outside the town, all the schoolchildren were on the road, going home from school, and I immediately became tense all over again, this time anticipating that one would grab my handlebars like a child had the day we rode into Swaziland. I didn't want a repeat of that. Man, how I hated this. I was shaking and told Dean that as soon as a TK&A sag vehicle came by, I had to get off the road. I was so upset that it was unsafe for me to be on my bike. Within half an hour, I gave in to my fears and rode into Umtata as a sagger. I had never in my life been in the minority like I was that day, and it's not a feeling I wish to experience again. I know Ruth (the only lady cyclist who had ridden every mile so far) rode the entire 114 miles alone that day. She's one tough and lucky lady. I envied her. I just couldn't do it.

That evening when Teresa and I decided to walk a couple blocks to get bottled water for the next day, we were met by an armed guard who escorted us to the store. He radioed back after we made our purchases and another guard joined us. They both escorted us back to our campground, which was enclosed by a fence with a locked gate. Umtata, Nelson Mandela's birthplace, is apparently still a really rough town.

That evening, I wrote another email home.

Date: 2 Mar 2000
To: Craig and Bess
Subject: Wussy wussy

I'm really upset with myself for being such a chicken. I have never felt like this anywhere else. Maybe it's because of my limited experience, but others don't seem to let it bother them like I do. Dean was uncomfortable today, but he would have gone on. I want to be careful and feel safe, but on the other hand, I don't want to be a big coward. I think I'm going to be very glad when we leave Africa. The scenery is beautiful here, but that's it. At least I tried today. More than 120 others didn't even ride because they were scared. Just getting this off my chest so I can feel better. You guys are my sounding board. Sorry.

The ride out of Umtata was uneventful, and we toured the rest of South Africa without incident. In fact, it was quite enjoyable. Once we left the Transkei area, we rode along the coast often and took in the gorgeous views of sandy beaches and crashing waves. I rode with different cyclists each day, always talking of things that kept my mind occupied. There were no more scares or threats. By the time we got to Capetown, I looked back and wondered if I had over-reacted. Probably, since Ruth had managed to ride all of Africa alone. But what was done, was done, and I had to learn from it. I needed to develop self-confidence and trust more. I didn't know how else to explain it. The language barrier and the fact that I was unaccustomed to the Africans' way of life were probably my biggest obstacles. I really wished I could have gone back and done it all over. We really did meet a lot of friendly people, like the vendors who provided our meals. But I blew it and would have to live with my own inadequacies. Hopefully, I wouldn't let it happen again. Only time would tell if I could grow from the experience.

CHAPTER 5
Greece: Survival

March 17 to March 23

3,848.1 miles to date

"He who learns to sag today lives to ride tomorrow."—Ed Lang

Tom, one of Al's sagger friends, loading bikes for other saggers

5

GREECE

Our flight from Cape Town to Athens, Greece, was uneventful but delayed. This seemed to be a constant. Every time we flew, we were delayed by an hour to 16 hours. That caused us to arrive at the next place later than scheduled, which usually shortened our time to sightsee. We were due to arrive in Athens in the wee hours of the morning, but when we landed it was 10 a.m. By the time all our bags and bikes were accounted for, it was 3:30 p.m. This was our only layover day in Athens, and by the time I got to the hotel, changed a tire, showered and ate, it was time for bed. So I signed up for a bus tour of the city for the next day, arranged by Denise, that allowed us to see the Acropolis, then took us to our next night's destination, all for a small fee. I just couldn't be in Athens and not see the Parthenon.

I was starting to understand why some riders always went off route. There weren't many things I'd give up a day of riding to see, but the Parthenon was one of them. I had seen the pictures, of course, and I really wanted to see it in person. Besides, I didn't know if I'd ever get back that way. It was awesome. To stand next to the remains of a 2,000-year-old building made me understand better what the people from centuries ago had to do to build something like that. They didn't have machines to do the heavy work. They didn't have computers to help them draw up plans.

It was hard to imagine people back then building something of that magnitude, on top of a hill, no less. The fact that parts of it had survived all those years is amazing. To look out over modern Athens exhilarated me. Cities have never turned me on, but this one was neat. There was white marble everywhere. It looked so clean, so crowded, yet so amazing. I was glad I did the tour.

49

This was the beginning of my interest in history. My sister Bess always tried to interest me in the history of the world, but I just didn't care, until I stood beside those ancient ruins. It brought it all to life for me.

I rode out of our Epidavros campground with Ed the next morning. When we stopped for a break, we ended up at a coffee shop in Lerna, the home of Hercules. The café owner told us all about Hercules and how proud he was to have his café next to Lake Lerna, where Hercules had slain the serpent. He treated us to coffee and a sweet, all the while testing our knowledge of the Greek myths. He seemed to be having more fun than we were and didn't want to let us go, but we explained that we had much more riding to do yet that day. And he spoke very good English as did many of the people in Greece, which made our visit all the more enjoyable. It was a beautiful ride as we passed many hilltop towns that have existed for centuries. It just boggled my mind that people centuries ago hauled large rocks up the mountains to build a town. I was later told that towns were built high on the hilltops so the people could see their enemies coming.

The next morning, Ed and I rode out of Tiros Arcadia: an immediate climb, and then up and down along the water to a town called Leonidio, another ancient city. Doors of buildings opened right onto the streets, which were so narrow only one small car could get through. I was happy to see that the people of Greece had not torn down ancient buildings to accommodate larger highways. A wide two-lane road approached the town and, almost immediately, it narrowed to a one-lane street lined by rock buildings. I fell in love with Leonidio for this reason. I could just imagine how it had been with no cars 2,000 years ago. On the other side of town, the road widened to two lanes again. It was like a time warp. We saw this Old World tradition time and again throughout Greece and Italy.

After crossing the Parnona Mountains, we ended up in Sparti. From there, I could see another mountain range we'd be crossing the next day, and it had an awful lot of white stuff on it. I hoped we would cross under the snow level.

This turned out to be another sleepless night. It was normal for me to sleep a couple hours, get up and find a bathroom, lay awake for a couple hours, then doze off just before it was time to get up. Suffering with a cold and major congestion for a couple days made it all the worse. I left camp later than usual because I just didn't feel good, and sure enough, we started a 20-kilometer climb right out of town. It started sprinkling, turned to spitting snow, then real snow that stuck to the sides of the road. The higher we went, the colder it got. Not pleasant at all. I rode all the way to checkpoint alone and was ready to bag it but couldn't get a sag ride, so Brenda and I took off down the other side of this mountain, only to end up walking the first 3 kilometers because visibility was so bad and the roads were slick. That day, Win fell and broke his femur, and Phil fell and ended up with a hematoma on his thigh. It was bad. I never ride in conditions like that at home. Near the bottom, we ran into heavy rain. I was sick, cold and wet, and lucky I didn't catch pneumonia like several other riders had. The conditions seemed to test the "survival of the fittest." I don't know how I lucked out. Guess my stubbornness was a factor.

About 20 kilometers from our camp in Gialova, the heavens opened up again, and Brenda and I decided we'd had enough. So we waited for a sag vehicle at a local gas station. When we got to camp, the gear trucks weren't even unloaded at 5 p.m. Ed and Willma offered me a bed in town a ways away, but I declined. It was too much effort to dig for specific items needed only for the night. My gear was packed for camping, not for running off to a hotel. I pitched my tent under a tree on the gravel street. My chosen pad had the least amount of water standing on it. There were only fifteen tents out that night, but for me, it worked fine. After all, we were tough.

Two days later we camped in Olympia, home of the first Greek Olympics back in 10 B.C. How awesome it was to walk the ruins. Ed, Willma, Peter and I toured the grounds extensively, taking in the wonder of it all. To see sites so old preserved for future generations was the highlight of Greece for me.

CHAPTER 6
Italy:
Ancient and
Recent History

March 24 to April 13

4,929.0 miles to date

"Happiness is being married to your best friend."—Phil Gravink

Phil and Shirley Gravink

Willma and Ed Lang with Gary (dutiful husband changing flat tire) and Cheryl Minor

6

ITALY

After taking the train from Olympia to Patra, we set sail on a ferry to Bari, Italy. We went from wet and cold camping to a cramped closet-size room with four bunk beds on the ferry, hotter than hot. No wonder so many people were sick all the time.

Southern Italy was my favorite part of the country. There were rock fences everywhere. I never wondered where the rocks came from to build all those castles, but after riding there, I knew. They just picked them up out of the fields. They reminded me of the rocks we had to pick up on the farm, which were dropped by receding glaciers. Most were fist- to head-size rocks with several boulders thrown in.

On our ride into Scalea, I got to sing in 14 tunnels. Wow, the acoustics were great. But it was in Scalea where laundry became a real issue. Ever since we left home, finding Laundromats, as we know them, had been a real chore. In Costa Rica, I had paid $12 to have about six pieces laundered when I couldn't find a do-it-yourself Laundromat. I had been quoted a reasonable price and time, I thought, but obviously I misunderstood. When my clothes were finally delivered to my hotel, what could I do but pay it and try to do better next time? In Chile, do-it-yourself Laundromats became even more rare, and by the end of Greece I had resorted to rinsing a few things out by hand if I got desperate. When we had the layover day in Scalea I thought, "Now would be a good time to get all my clothes washed since almost every piece I own is dirty." But, there were no self-serve Laundromats! In fact, we could only find two Laundromats in the whole city, and they only did your laundry for you.

Several cyclists left their clothes early the layover day morning and were promised the laundry would be done by 6 p.m. After walking the streets of the city and accomplishing other chores, Willma and I checked back just in case our clothes were done early. No, and the time was pushed to 7 p.m. More cyclists had found this Laundromat, and they were busier than usual. Now in Italy, everything closes down from 12:30 or 1:00 until 4:30 or 5:00. Siesta time, I guess. We checked again just before dinner and were told 9 p.m. There were three huge piles of clothing lying in the middle of the floor that hadn't been washed yet.

Hundreds of biker shorts, jerseys and socks were in these piles. We just stood there with our mouths open. How in the world would they know whose were whose? Cheryl saw three of her items, each in a different pile. And they told us this time it would be 5 a.m. I was about to have a tizzy fit. I had one t-shirt and the clothes I was wearing in my possession. Everything else was in those piles. If our clothes weren't ready by breakfast time, it would mean we'd have to stay behind to collect them and probably carry them on our bikes. Impossible. Willma and I were at wit's end, and Ed just didn't understand why we were so uptight. His solution was to go buy more clothes. Not an option on my end. I vowed that this would be the last time I gave my clothes to someone else to do.

The next morning at 4:30 a.m., Ed went to pick up our clothes, and lo and behold, they were ready. First thing we did when he got back was go through our packages to see if we got our own clothes. I was missing my favorite scarf and Willma was missing two shirts and a sheet. At breakfast everyone asked around, and most of us found our missing items. Biggest bummer was that it cost us $20 for our laundry. Definitely the last time I did that.

Our ride along the coast was to the top of every hill to ride through the "old town," then back to the ocean to go through today's modern tourist town, then back up and down. Beautiful coastline. Six days into Italy, we camped at Paestum near the ruins of a 600 B.C. Greek settlement about a mile square. It had been taken over by the Romans later, then abandoned and later re-excavated. Very similar to the Olympia remains. Greek-style temples and amphitheaters were everywhere. I didn't even know something like that existed in Italy. Boy was I getting an education, and my little sister was probably saying, "It's about time."

The next day we rode into Pompeii. I didn't think it could get any better. A whole city unearthed from volcanic ash! I was in heaven. I had always read about this but had no idea of the magnitude of Pompeii. I stayed an extra day to tour it again. I then took a train to Rome where I met my friend Laura from Idaho. Imagine sitting at a dinner table with a view of the Roman Colosseum. Never in my life did I ever think I'd see something like this. The next day, Laura and I took a train to the medieval city of San Gimignano. We thought we were really branching out to see something unique. Little did I know that Odyssey would ride near or through several of these towns in the next couple of weeks. But we took a leisurely walk through it that I never had time for while I was riding, so it was worth it. The three days I spent with Laura were action-packed as we tried to see as much as possible. I never did make it to the Vatican, but there's always tomorrow.

The day I left Laura to ride to camp and catch up with the rest of the group it was raining again. I had to ride through Rome alone, on wet cobblestone streets with lots of traffic. But I did it. I never would have attempted that three months earlier. I felt like I was becoming more self-assured.

The first day out of Rome, we camped in Assisi. It was another partially walled city on top of a hill. Riding out of Assisi was all downhill and of course, it had rained so the roads were wet. But 70 miles later, after much up and down, we ended up on top of a big hill in Urbino, birthplace of Raphael.

It was downhill for 10 kilometers out of Urbino with a whopping 8,000-plus feet of elevation gain via San Marino on our way to Caprese Michelangelo, birthplace of Michelangelo. I kept seeing this impressive castle off in the distance, never dreaming we'd climb all the way up there just to ride down the other side. San Marino was the smallest country we visited on our trip around the world, and I can't say it was worth the climb up there just to say we'd been there. The ride out of Caprese Michelangelo was mostly downhill as we headed into Florence, home of the "David" sculpture, the Duomo of Florence and Giotti's Tower.

The next day took us to Pisa and the Leaning Tower. Wow! I had no idea it was that big. Of course, we rode into Pisa in the rain, and water was standing everywhere. My good friends Phil and Shirley invited me to stay in a small cabin that had six beds, and I took them up on it. I told myself this was an OK time to pay for a room, when there was no dry place to pitch a tent and I could take my entire bag with me. At dinner, we celebrated Shirley's birthday and Phil made a toast I'll never forget. "Happiness is being married to your best friend." They are truly a neat couple.

From Pisa we went to Levanto, home of some of the steepest vineyards I've ever seen. It was here that Odyssey made history. Our gear trucks were impounded and not allowed to move off the premises due to insurance problems. We didn't know about this until we got to the next camp, and we never really understood the whole situation. For the riders it meant no access to anything other than what we had on our bikes. Each rider had a compartment roughly 17x17x34 inches for all his or her gear. If it didn't fit in there, you had to carry it. I had purposely lightened my bags that day and even left my PocketMail device in the gear truck because I knew we had lots of hills and I didn't want to carry any more than necessary. While sitting around waiting for the trucks (that we later learned would not be coming that evening), I was handwriting notes about the day so I wouldn't forget. Dick came by and said, "You do know how to write." He had only seen me typing on my PocketMail. I took it with me all the time, except this once. I would always be typing away while standing in one of the many lines we had to endure daily. No one ever saw me without it. Maryke also came by while I was using pencil and paper and said that was the best thing to ever happen to me. "Forces you to relax," she said, when in reality it was causing me more stress. Yes, I had become addicted to my little machine. It was my contact with the outside world. We stayed in hotels in Geneva (Genoa) that night, right across the street from the statue of Cristoforo Columbo, Christopher Columbus. That was his birthplace.

In spite of the inconvenience, we persevered the next day to arrive in Menton, France, only to find out that we still had no gear trucks. So we were bused from Menton ahead to Nice, France, and given another hotel room. We had by that time worn the same clothes for two solid days. While some riders were getting testy, the rest of us looked at it as an adventure. But let me tell you, I was really happy when I got my PocketMail back after three days without it. Hallelujah! The TK&A staff had to cut all our locks off, bag any loose stuff and label it with our names, and haul it to us that third day. The trucks still could not move from Levanto. But at least we had our belongings.

I was amazed by all I had seen in those three weeks in Italy. Things I had heard about or seen pictures of came to life: Pompei, Rome, the Leaning Tower of Pisa, the Duomo of Florence and walled cities. It's not the same as seeing the pictures in history books. I had to see it in person to feel the enormity of it all. When I wrote to Bess and explained how all this had affected me, she was pleased. I told her my sudden appreciation of history was just a flash bulb that went off, not a light bulb that would stay on and burn continuously. She wrote back letting me know she approved, and at the same time giving me the what-for.

Date: April 2000

A flash bulb and not a light bulb—I like that. Perfect description although I must admit I am a little disappointed. I was hoping this would be the start of something new and different for you. But I guess I'll just have to be content knowing at least you can appreciate the history of things while you're "there." So no life-changing experience, but you have to admit history is neat.

I think this trip has been very good for you. You are seeing things that you have never been exposed to before, and you have had to deal with things that you have never had to deal with before: you are not always in control. That, in itself, is new for you, and that's a good thing. I want you to learn to relax and let others have the responsibility of making the decisions. Put your Post-it notes and your lists of things to do away and just sit back and go with the flow. I am not being nasty (have to get my jabs in once in a while). I want to see you enjoy life and not have to be working so hard at two and three jobs to get what you want. I like that you have come to terms with your own limitations and are willing to hitch a ride once in a while. I'm sure the decision to do that hasn't always been easy, but see, you don't have to push yourself to the edges of endurance to have fun.

Sorry if it seems I come down so hard on you sometimes, but I think you push yourself too far at times. I cheer a little whenever I read you hitched a ride. I don't want to hear about you getting sick again because the ride was so tough or the heat got to you. I say these things because I care too much and have plans for us when you get home. There, I sound like a mother hen again, but tough. I'll keep saying it until I know you're home safe and sound. I really do miss talking to you in person. A phone call when you are in D.C. would make my day.

CHAPTER 7

France, Spain, Gibraltar and Portugal: Building Bridges

April 14 to May 12

6,254.2 miles to date

"Growing old is mandatory; growing up is optional."
—Quipped by Bob Mack

*Al riding down a cable near
Bariloche, Argentina*

*Peter Bolton, Alan Bouchard, Bill Sokolik, Steve Alexander, Russ Carter, Neil Van Steenbergen,
Rip Steutzel and Ron Smith at a rainy dinner in Cordoba*

7

FRANCE, SPAIN, GIBRALTAR AND PORTUGAL

Something happened about this time and I don't know what. Maybe I relaxed or started feeling more positive about myself. It seems I started having a lot more fun trying new things and mixing more with people.

My first ride with Charlie was in France on the 119.9-mile day into Carcasonne. We met about halfway through the day and rode the rest of the way into camp, talking about gardens and flowers all the way. The quiet backcountry roads allowed us to ride side by side. He was the first guy I'd ever met who was really into gardening and appreciated plants like I do, so we hit if off pretty well. I knew who he was but had never said more than "Hi" the previous three and a half months of the trip. My only real encounter with him had been in Kokstad, South Africa, when I just happened to be sitting at the same dinner table. He and the guys were talking about how the wrong Charlie had been reprimanded for leaving camp before sunrise. I knew this Charlie left early, often before breakfast, and that's why I rarely saw him except in the dinner line. We thought it was pretty funny that TK&A leader, Tim, didn't even know exactly who the culprit was, just that his name was Charlie. That day into Carcasonne was the beginning of a good friendship. Throughout the rest of the year, we rode together often and visited many botanical gardens.

Because of the big-city riding we did so often, I tried to latch onto someone I thought was a pretty good navigator. Among those I tried to follow were Ed and Willma, Beth and/or Teresa, and Charlie. Even though Charlie got lost a lot, he didn't let it bother him, and I felt safe knowing he wouldn't leave me behind. I always knew I'd be OK if I followed these riders. This is also about the time I started riding fairly consistently with the same few people. I had finally found other riders who liked to ride a fairly consistent speed, not overly fast and not turtle speed. We also stopped periodically to eat, find a bush or rest aching muscles.

In Carcasonne, the tour leader held a big meeting in which several riders aired concerns. Unfortunately, it became a finger-pointing session. Many riders were extremely upset that we didn't have a doctor "on board," sagging policies seemed inconsistent, and general day-to-day living on the trip wasn't what they expected. I was embarrassed at one point and just wondered why these people couldn't get a life. It put TK&A on the defensive, and nothing ever changed. I also wondered why some of these people didn't go home if it was that bad for them. Meetings like that one only divided the group and accomplished very little in the long run. I had learned long ago to go with the flow and that what is…is. I didn't foresee TK&A changing anything.

It was there in that meeting that I stood up and asked people if they had any interest in forming an Odyssey choir. I felt we needed some positive vibes in the group and that maybe a choir could help unify us rather than divide us. Boy, was I getting brave or what? Actually, several people signed the sheet I passed around. Later I found out that many were interested in a choir but only wanted to listen. That was OK. We would need an audience, too.

After a layover day in Carcasonne, we headed out in the rain to Ax les Thermes. It was Easter Sunday and turned out to be my absolute worst day of the trip. We got wet on the way to breakfast and were already chilled before starting the day's ride. Right out of town we started gaining elevation, and got colder and wetter. It even snowed on top. I was totally unprepared for the conditions and ended up sitting by the side of the road, crying, after my third unsuccessful attempt at getting a sag ride with TK&A. I don't think I could have carried enough clothes that day, and I realized my rain gear was not acceptable for the conditions in which we had to ride. I had lots of clothes on but I was soaked to the bone and equally chilled. Every van that went by was already full. I'd get the same response every time: "You'll have to wait for the next one." I was on the verge of hypothermia and frostbite but couldn't get out of the weather. Crying helped though. I actually warmed up and persevered onward until I came to a restaurant where a lot of riders were holed up. After they saw how bad I was, I was taken into camp.

The day after Ax les Thermes was one of my best. It was cold, but I was prepared (dry), and we rode up and over the Pyrenees, through Andorra and into Spain. We went from one extreme to the other, cold with lots of clothes on to 70 degrees on the other side. It was really hard to dress for that kind of riding, and we always ended up carrying lots of what we took off.

A couple days after we rode through Andorra, we ended up in Barcelona. We had two layover days there, and I finally got the nerve to start the Odyssey choir I had wanted ever since I signed up for the trip. Up until a couple of weeks before, I had been afraid people would think it was a stupid idea, so I didn't pursue it. The sign-up sheet from Carcasonne was encouraging, though, so I thought I'd call a rehearsal and see who showed up. We started with 14, and with each rehearsal we gained a couple more. It finally leveled out around 23 regular members and was to become a very unifying part of Odyssey in the months to come. We just didn't know it yet. I always felt so energized after rehearsal. Guess I missed my music teaching job back home a little.

Also, in Barcelona, we had extra time to socialize, and I got to know several teacher types really well one afternoon. We all happened to be sitting at a table reading or catching up on correspondence. It started out really quiet, like being in a library. Soon it deteriorated into a typical high school study hall frenzy with spit wads and giggling. There was Dick, a coffee shop and bookstore owner; Rip, a real "quiet" character; Neil, a retired teacher who had seen it all; Florida Bill, a teacher of severely mentally handicapped kids; and myself. Once the fun began, we just gave up and talked.

I also started playing cards with Alan, Margherita and Nancy that day. We would spend many hours the rest of the year at this pastime. We left Barcelona by a 14-hour bus ride to Gibraltar, so we had lots more time to talk and play cards. I wondered, "Where have these people been the past four months?" and "Why did it take me so long to find them?" Guess I had been too focused on doing every mile. Once I got over that, I really started to have more fun.

On that bus ride, we had several stops to stretch and use bathroom facilities. At one stop, there just happened to be a playground. Margherita and I played on the teeter-totters, swings and slide. What a release of tension. (Others thought we were crazy, but we didn't care.) We were having fun and getting the kinks out.

Our bus ride took us to Gibraltar and another layover day. From there, we rode back along the coast and eventually up to Granada. I actually convinced Charlie to eat breakfast at camp so I could ride with him. It was only a 50-mile day, short by most standards, so we didn't need to get a particularly early start. This was the day I learned about ketchup sandwiches, Charlie's staple. He really did squeeze ketchup on bread and eat it.

The next morning, we woke up to rain and the temperature dropped as we were eating breakfast. Here we go again. I remembered Ax les Thermes, where I had suffered from near hypothermia and frostbite, and I didn't want a repeat, so I wimped out and took a bus, only to have the sun come out midmorning and have the day turn beautiful. Who was to know? I quit trying to predict the weather. I berated myself on the entire bus ride to Cordoba. I hated myself, and Ed and Willma kept saying, "What is done, is done." Yeah, but I was missing a great ride. So when we arrived in town, I rode the route backwards as far as time allowed and then cooled down with a slow easy ride with Charlie through fields of flowers for an hour or so before dinner. I felt better after having at least been able to ride some of that gorgeous route through the olive orchards. You can imagine the looks I got from some of the riders as I passed them going in the wrong direction. I just waved and smiled.

We had a layover day in Cordoba. After sightseeing a large part of the day, I played Scrabble with Peter and Alan, an activity that would soon become even more frequent than the card games.

At dinner that night in Cordoba, we had tables around the pool with white linen tablecloths and real flowers for a centerpiece. Don't know how, but I ended up at a table with eight guys. Steve was the "ring leader" and Neil, the "straight man" who kept us in stitches. I laughed more than I ate. When it started to sprinkle, bald-headed Steve put his white linen napkin on his head and the rest followed. I was momentarily embarrassed, but when I noticed Jim with a chair on his head at another table, I figured my dinner companions weren't so bad. We finished off the evening with more Scrabble in our tents until it became too dark to see.

On the next day's ride into Seville, I rode with Fast Fred. Another retired teacher, he was fast on his bike, and I wanted to get some pointers from him. He really worked me hard, but I learned a lot. We had another layover day there, in Seville, and I brought out the Balderdash cards. (I came prepared with all kinds of things to do: music, brass mouthpieces, cards, Balderdash. Peter had the pocket Scrabble game, although I ended up buying my own in Australia.) Back home, I'm often referred to as the recreation director. I had just been waiting for people to come to me, I guess. I'm glad I finally became self-confident enough to approach them first. Alan, Peter, Linda, Charmaine, Margherita and I played and laughed like a bunch of kids. Boy was I having fun, not only riding, but getting to know people on a one-to-one basis. It was what I had hoped for.

Most of the time I had been riding with Ed and Willma, a really neat couple, really upbeat and real go-getters. I know I first hooked up with those two because of their ever-present smiling faces and positive attitudes. Willma became my confidant later on. And she was always giving us a laugh. One day at breakfast she was complaining about her helmet hurting her head. She took it off and, lo and behold, she had a clothespin stuck in her hair. Another morning at breakfast, she came in and sat down beside a fellow who had on the exact same rain jacket as Ed. Ed and I were already seated and wondered why Willma didn't sit with us. I asked her later what her problem was and she answered simply, "I got up." Ed gave her a hard time about what she had probably said to the other fellow before she realized it wasn't Ed. I loved riding with the two of them. We took lots of bush breaks, ate often and jabbered the whole day.

By the time we were ready to go back to the States for two weeks, I had truly become one of the Odyssey gang. I got to know several riders just because their family or friends read my daily journal on my Webpage and would ask me to deliver a message or just say "Hi." Gave me an excuse to talk to others without just making small talk. The choir really boosted my self-image. I had something to offer Odyssey, and I could be a positive influence. I now had the choir, the Scrabble crew, the card-playing bunch and a Balderdash bunch, as well as my regular riding buddies. I was in heaven and had finally found a happy medium. I was still a type A+ person and not capable of mellowing out, but I had become a little less obsessed with being macho. That didn't seem to be top priority anymore. Some of us are just slow learners.

CHAPTER 8
United States and Canada: An Ego Boost

May 13 to June 5

7,413.4 miles to date

"You talk to your birds, and I'll talk to mine."—Mark Bovee

Al feeding the geese just off the road

8

United States and Canada

We flew from Lisbon, Portugal, to Washington D.C. on May 12 and with the time change, most of us had been up for 21 hours. We were zombies. And to top it off, our hostel room was sweltering because the air conditioning didn't work and there were eight to 12 of us in a unit. Lack of sleep seemed to be the theme of the year. I was awake from 4 a.m. to 7 a.m. and drenched in sweat. No way had I made up for my sleep deficit.

I met several family members of riders that first evening and morning after our arrival in D.C. They knew me only through the Webpage and were really appreciative of all I'd done to keep them posted about Odyssey happenings. Several riders complained to me jokingly because I had made them look bad by writing every day, when some of them only wrote home once or twice a month. My Webpage had become the only portal for information for some of their family members.

My two sisters, Bess and Barb, and Barb's daughter, Deanna, drove to D.C. from Ohio to visit me for two days. This was a pleasant surprise, as I didn't think they'd want to drive that far just for two days. But I was really glad to see them. A lot of riders decided to go home for the five days we were in D.C., and some decided not to return until Odyssey left for Canada. I had planned on spending the time alone, filling prescriptions and catching up on laundry, bike maintenance, repairs to clothes and equipment, correspondence and maybe some sleep.

First thing we did was exchange packages from home with stuff to be sent home. I had lots of homemade cookies to take with me. They handed me an envelope of letters, checks and cash that my good friend, Fred, from Kansas, had collected from various Webpage readers and other friends. I had not felt deprived all year, as I knew my limitations and tried to live within them. But the Fun Fund was awesome. There were checks and letters from people who only knew me through the Webpage. I must say when Craig asked me if I wanted a Webpage soon after I signed up for Odyssey, I said, "What for? Who wants to read about me?" He finally talked me into it so I could let Web readers know all about Odyssey. OK, but I thought it was a waste of time.

Before I left home in December, I spent weeks trying to find the perfect way to send daily emails home so he could update the Webpage. I knew that the Internet access would not be reliable. I settled on the Sharp TM-20 with PocketMail that transmits by phone. I typed my daily journal on this device, talking about everything from where we were and how we got there, to accommodations, food, weather, happenings in the group, and every little thing I did. It was my personal journal. Soon after the ride began, people latched onto my Webpage and became obsessed with reading it every day.

Craig often had people write to him when I missed a day, due to lousy phones or whatever, and ask why I hadn't written. When he went on vacation and notified the Web readers that he'd be gone for a week, some wrote and told him he couldn't go. Others made comments like, "No updates for 12 days???????????? Oooooooooohhhhhhhhhhh!!!! We will miss the postings and will look forward to them when you return."

Another reader commented, "Don't you know you're not allowed to take any time off until Al's trip is over?" And another wrote, "I would like to thank Craig for his diligence in keeping the Website current. When he is going to be away he lets us know ahead of time, which is a very nice touch. The warning allows us to prepare for missing our 'daily dose of Al.'" So by May I had quite a following. Not only did I write for myself, I answered questions from time to time and relayed messages to other riders.

I was very regimented in my daily writing. Because we rarely stayed in one spot longer than one night, I couldn't remember what happened or where I was the day before. I carried my PocketMail everywhere I went. I wrote in shower lines, dinner lines, while I played games, and anywhere that I had five minutes to spare. I became known as 'PocketMail Al' and people often commented about how it was always in use. A couple riders came by my tent one night in Canada and took a picture of me sitting there typing. They were as obsessed as I was.

I transmitted daily if I could find phones that worked. That is how I sent regular emails to Craig and Bess, too. One night in Paestum, Italy, I walked a mile to find a phone—and that wasn't the only time. Craig proofread and posted my daily journal and forwarded questions and comments from readers to me. When a Webpage reader asked him exactly what he did, he replied with the following explanation.

The whole process begins with Al, who took with her a Sharp TM-20, which is about the size of a small address book. This connects to an email service called PocketMail. With that, she writes her thoughts and observations daily, and periodically emails them back to me.

I use Adobe PageMill software to organize and generate the HTML code for the Website. Once I receive Al's email, I start by opening the current Website page and beginning a new section with the appropriate date.

Then I read the journal for content, breaking it up into related and easy-to-read paragraphs, correcting spelling, punctuation, typos, etc., and editing the text, as needed, for clarification. I also insert various technical editing, which you never see, but which helps "shape" the general appearance of the text.

I then take Al's riding distance in kilometers and plug that into a spreadsheet which computes and tabulates miles, cumulative distance, number of cycling days, cumulative daily average cycling distance, and number of century rides. Then for the Webpage, I format Al's riding distance and elevation figures, and include the "Posted Distance" for scheduled riding days when Al rode only part way, or not at all.

After that, I begin Internet searches to locate other Websites about the cities and points of interest referenced in Al's journals, attaching appropriate links as available.

Al's photographs are sent for processing to PhotoWorks (a.k.a. Seattle Film Works), which makes them available to me electronically. Then I build a Webpage including the picture, a caption and date, and relative links.

Once I have finished, I run the Adobe spell-checker to help correct errors I may have missed. Then I "view" the updated Website through my browser, so I can see the site as you will. If needed, I make further changes or corrections before the update is ready for posting to the World Wide Web.

Additional email chores include a confirmation to Al notifying her of which emails I received (so she can re-transmit anything that went astray), updating my notification list (including an acknowledgement to each new subscriber), forwarding comments and questions to Al, and finally sending out the update notification to all of you.

All of these activities consume an average of two hours per day, and often more, so it's nice to know that so many of you are enjoying the results. And that is how the Website is produced.

Even I had no idea of how much work was involved. So I asked Craig three questions: Did you ever think my Webpage would be so popular? No. Did you ever think the Webpage would be this much work? No. Are you sorry you talked me into having a Webpage? No. Whew!

So the envelope delivered by my sister contained some of the nicest things people had ever said to me. I was flattered to think anyone would ever want to read what I wrote and even more flattered to think they'd donate to a fund for me to go out and play. I was also flattered that Fred would go out of his way to organize something like that. Unbeknownst to me, he had planned to fly out to D.C. and deliver it himself but had to go to a wedding in Colorado. So he mailed it to Bess to bring. Awesome.

My sisters stayed in Gaithersburg, Maryland, and took the Metro to D.C. each day. I went back and forth with them and stayed in their motel. On the metro, I noticed a poster with a poem entitled "Don't Think" by Judith Viorst. I had to copy it down because it was so fitting for Willma and me.

Don't think rivers
Don't think fountains
Don't think mountain stream or creeks
Don't think pools or ponds or oceans
Don't think lakes and don't think leaks
Don't think wells or wet or water
Don't think showers
Don't think springs
Don't think moist or damp or rainy
Don't think hurricanes or things
That drizzle, dribble, drip, drop, flood, or flow
When there's no bathroom and you gotta go.

The four of us spent those two days sightseeing and covering as much ground on foot as possible in D.C. Ed and Willma invited us to breakfast Sunday to celebrate their 40th wedding anniversary. I felt honored to share in that celebration with them. The last evening we girls were together, we looked at the scrapbooks Bess had started. That's her thing, and it's definitely not mine. All year long I had to save stubs, labels and receipts, such as exorbitant laundry bills, while she collected cartoons and did some editorializing. By the end of the year, she would have seven scrapbooks of pictures and memorabilia for me. What a job!

Bess, Barb and Deanna left the morning of the third day after taking me shopping to replace some worn-out clothes. I had the rest of the day to do all the things I needed to do in the United States before heading back overseas. I really wanted to get my bike overhauled, but every bike shop was already overbooked. I rode my bike all over D.C. trying to accomplish these tasks, and for the second time that year, I realized I could ride in a big city by myself and not get lost or frustrated. I had come a long way in that respect. It was such a good feeling.

A biker friend whom I had met on the Wyoming ride in 1999 lived in Ellicott City, Maryland, and met me at the Silver Springs Metro station to take me to his community band rehearsal one night. What a fun time that was. Then he drove me all the way back to D.C. yet that night. I was continually amazed that people were going, what seemed to me, out of their way. I didn't know if I deserved it.

My fourth day in D.C. was spent taking a tour bus to Mt. Vernon. I spent that evening with Dean and Judy and some of their family members playing Balderdash. Their family had been following my Webpage, too.

The last day in D.C., I rode back out to Mt. Vernon with Mark and Sandy and staff member, Randy. I talked to the ducks and geese along the river, as they are my favorite critters. Our bike path took us right under the flight path of planes landing at and leaving Washington National

Airport. At one point during the ride, Mark growled "Vrooooooom" in a throaty voice, and we about fell off our bikes with laughter. Then he looked at me and said, "You talk to your birds, and I'll talk to mine." I was glad we rode that day because our bikes needed some adjustments after the international flight.

It was then time to repack and get back on the road. Those few days had been good as I accomplished a lot and felt ready to continue on. Since I had talked on my Webpage about my inability to get my bike overhauled, readers knew of this slight problem. It just so happened that Sylvia, a Webpage reader with whom I had corresponded several times about different things, offered to take me into a Lancaster, Pennsylvania, bike shop when the tour group got there, just two days out of D.C. She ended up meeting me in camp that night, taking me and my bike to the bike shop, bringing me back to camp, and picking me up the next morning to collect my bike and pay for repairs. She didn't even know me.

I felt special and honored that some one would even do that. All these Webpage readers were putting me on a real high. It felt good to be producing something that people wanted and liked. All through high school and college I had been told my writing was worthless. Now I didn't dare skip a day for any reason. Too many people were expecting something every day. I had created monsters out there.

A TK&A employee from the Seattle home office joined us for a short time right after D.C. As I rode into camp the first night, this fellow, whom I had never seen before, came up to me and asked, "You're Al, aren't you?" Whoa, I asked, how did he know me? He said, "You're wearing purple, aren't you?" He knew me from what I had written on my Webpage. Kind of spooky.

I followed Teresa into New York City a couple of days later. I wasn't quite ready to do that alone. We rode right by the twin towers of the World Trade Center and past Central Park to our hostel accommodations on the edge of Harlem. Never in my life did I ever dream I'd ride my bike in New York City. What a rush!

I walked through Central Park with Organist Bill the next day and visited the Lincoln Center. I ended up seeing three different Broadway shows, one each day, thanks to the generosity of my Webpage readers. It was awesome, to be sure.

Our staff people got to know us rather well, including our quirks and idiosyncrasies. I think we felt most comfortable around some of them because we saw them every day, when often we wouldn't see some riders more than once in a week. One particularly hard day, after lots of big hills and lots of strong headwind, I came into the final checkpoint at camp about five minutes before dinner was to be served, and my butt hurt. I had pushed so hard into the saddle I could hardly extricate myself from the seat. As I was trying to do so, I was chanting, "My butt, my butt, my butt," with my usual enthusiasm. The staff then informed me that the lady standing right near the table was there to see me. Turned out to be the grandmother of one of my students from school. Oh, my! Was I ever embarrassed! To someone who didn't know me, I probably sounded like a real dork. She and her husband were there to hand-deliver a care package of Power Bars and Nutella from their grandson, Alec. I was impressed. We talked a bit, and then I ran off to dinner.

My principal back in Idaho had written and asked me to call the school before the end of the school year. Well, that gave me about a week, so out in the boonies of Canada one day, I called from a pay phone and talked to him and several teachers. I didn't know it at the time, but he had been printing off my Webpage journal each week and passing it out in staff meetings, so they were all following me around the world. I had the impression when I left that they all thought I was crazy to give up a new, warm house and a good-paying job to ride my bike every day and camp out. Made me feel good to know they were interested.

One of my dear Idaho friends, Elizabeth, who had moved to Port Angeles, Washington just a year earlier, had planned to take a trip to Quebec that summer. After she had made arrangements, she noticed she'd be in Quebec when we were to be in Montreal. So she decided to rent a car and drive to Montreal to see me for an evening. Boy did we ever have a nonstop three-hour chat. We hardly took time to breathe.

I have to credit Elizabeth with giving me the courage to do the Odyssey bike trip. Way back in 1994, I tried to find someone to go to New Orleans with me while I attended a music convention. No one could go, and she told me then that if I always waited for someone to go with me, I wouldn't go very many places. But to the big city? I was petrified. However, I went, learned a lot about being in a big city alone, and had lots of stories to tell when I got home. Another friend told me when I returned that he thought I'd better take someone with me next time. But Elizabeth had given me the confidence to try traveling alone. My thanks to her.

Elizabeth's visit to Montreal capped off a glorious two weeks of meeting family and friends and those who believed in me. I was ready to head back to Europe for more adventure.

During those two weeks in the States, the choir had practiced several times, and we were getting pressured to perform. I kept saying that we had to get better and more polished before going public. The group was enthusiastic, and I was ecstatic that they were so dedicated to working hard, especially after a day's ride. I promised that by London, England, we would perform. That was only three weeks away.

CHAPTER 9
France:
ACCIDENT and the
Wheels of Fortune

June 6 to June 23

7,606.2 miles to date

*"Talk to me, girl, and tell me what happened.
THIS IS MY MOTHER VOICE SPEAKING."*
—*My sister Bess Robertson, reacting to my accident*

Dr. Charmaine Jones
tending to Al after her crash

Shirley Soth, Al and Stan Soth
saying goodbye in Quebec

9

FRANCE

Our trip back to Europe started on a very somber note. Two of our favorite, hard-working, very caring staff members, Stan and Shirley, were fired due to a difference of opinion with those higher in command and left us in Quebec the day we were to fly out. Then we had a four-hour wait at the airport—again. The only plus was that the choir made use of the time and practiced, in preparation for that promised London performance.

We flew out of Quebec to Paris, landing at 7 a.m., just in time to go sightseeing, except by the time we got rooms in the hotel, it was already early afternoon. Cheryl and I decided to spend the day touring as much of Paris as we could on foot and gave up the idea of taking a nap. We even took a night boat trip. We basically had no sleep in more than 36 hours.

TK&A offered a bus ride to the next camp for anyone wanting to stay in Paris and tour more. I did. I had barely touched the surface in one afternoon. I spent that first riding day touring the city with Brenda and Judy by bus, where they let you off to walk and you can catch the next tour bus that comes by and then go on to the next stop. If you didn't want to get off and walk around, you stayed on the bus. We arrived back at the hotel in time to catch the TK&A bus that took us to camp, just in time for dinner. Then off to bed I went. I was exhausted.

The next day's ride was 98 miles long, too long for the little sleep I'd had but relatively flat and very enjoyable. I took my time and had a great day. We were blessed with more heavy rain that night. I must say my Marmot Swallow tent was the best investment I ever made. Ninety-nine percent of the time, I stayed dry while other campers got horribly wet. Riders would complain every morning how they and everything in their tent was soaked, while I had been completely dry. This was the way it had been ever since the first rain we camped in way back in Chile. I loved my tent and praised it continually, even out loud sometimes. I just hated to put it away wet.

The next day I'll never forget. I started riding alone and then caught up with Ed and Willma. Cheryl came along, so I rode with her and her husband, Gary, for a while. We met up with five other riders and went to McDonald's for lunch. It was such a fun day of riding with all the different riders. But the best was yet to come. I headed out after lunch with Fast Fred and we later caught up to Peter, Gary, Mark and Sandy. We were cruising at speeds I didn't normally ride—for a long time. I finished the day with Alfred and Peter and was so proud that I had pushed hard enough to keep up with those I called the "Big Boys." But I was pooped. Still hadn't caught up on sleep and by dinnertime, I was dragging. No more oomph left at all.

The next morning, I got up later than I ever had and arrived at breakfast really late for me. We were to have a few hills that day, so Cheryl asked me if I wanted to ride with just her and go slowly. I jumped at the chance.

About 10 kilometers into the ride, I crashed big time. I hit the curb and went head first into a thick rock wall. It all happened so fast. All I remembered was thinking, "If I can just jump the curb." But it didn't happen.

Gary had left before us and took a wrong turn. He just happened to come across us right after I hit the wall. He would not let me move. My neck hurt, but I kept telling them that if they'd let me take my hair down, it would feel much better. No one would listen to me or let me move. Dr. Charmaine soon came along and tended to me until the ambulance arrived. I was so mad at myself. I was always so careful. How could this happen to me? It seemed like I was on that sidewalk forever.

The first thing I asked for out of my bike panniers was my PocketMail and identification. I was actually lying on the ground holding my PocketMail like it was my best friend. They could take away my bike but not my PocketMail. (Later, when the hospital personnel were to take me into surgery to sew up my knee, they wanted to put all my personal belongings in a bag. I asked about how safe it would be and they said they couldn't be responsible for anything not turned over to the hospital and locked up. That meant if I gave them my PocketMail, I wouldn't see it until I was released, and if I put it with my clothes, it could get stolen. I told Charmaine I had to have it accessible all the time, and she finally convinced them to let me hold it while in surgery.)

When the ambulance finally arrived, the medical folks put me in a neck brace and on a backboard and loaded me into the ambulance. Then we had to wait for a local doctor to come and examine me before they could take me to the hospital in Angers, France, about 20 miles from the scene of the accident. Charmaine went with me, and later a TK&A staff member showed up at the hospital with our temporary French-speaking staff member, Aymeric, son of our only French participant on Odyssey. Aymeric did all the translating at the hospital. Thank goodness. The hospital staff spoke very little English and most of us spoke even less French. Charmaine called my insurance and Craig. I was glad she was one of my friends.

At the hospital, we had to wait forever. They took x-rays, but it was Sunday and the orthopedic doctor was in surgery. When she finally looked at the x-rays, she decided to do a CTT scan. More waiting. I just wanted this to be over. I called all this waiting in "invisible lines." On Odyssey we waited in shower lines, breakfast and dinner lines, mechanic lines, check-in lines. But you always saw progress, slow though it might be at times. However, at the hospital, you never saw who might be "in front" of you and at times, you'd swear that invisible line wasn't even moving.

It was 7 p.m. when I got wheeled into surgery to sew up my knee. By this time, Charmaine, Aymeric and the staff person had returned to the riders and I was all alone. And I do mean alone. I couldn't communicate with anyone, and I hurt. The final diagnosis was three fractures, C1, C2 and C3, and a crack through the odontoid process (stabilizer) in my neck. Plus I had a goose egg on my forehead, a fat lip, and the deep gash in my knee that required 20 stitches inside and outside. I guess it was pretty bad—I never looked until the stitches came out. I was a mess, emotionally more than anything else. I wanted to cry but couldn't, so I typed in my PocketMail instead.

If you've never been in a situation like this, let me try to describe the feelings and thoughts that one has. First, the disbelief that an accident was going to happen, then the split-second belief that I could avoid the inevitable. I guess I decided it was time to remove a 2,000-year-old rock wall with my head, but alas, it is still standing and I'm a little worse for wear.

I felt the goose egg immediately and knew my head hurt. The instant fear of "How bad am I hurt?" went racing through my head. I never lost consciousness, so I was aware of all that was going on, for better or worse.

TK&A was pretty quick to arrive. I kept my wits and didn't go into shock, although when I knew there was blood, I had to make an effort to remain calm. While lying on the gurney, I had thoughts of: "Why me?" "Stupid me!" "Can this really be happening?" "What about the rest of the ride?" "Tomorrow is only 48 kilometers. I want to ride the short day." "Sure would love to get to move." "I just want to get this over with." "How thankful that it wasn't any worse than it was."

Craig's response was prompt and encouraging.

Date: 11 June 2000
Subject: Crash

Sorry to hear about your crash today and your related injuries. You probably know I spoke to Dr. Charmaine (about 5:40 your time), who gave me an update on your condition.

1. Think positively!! You are alive. You have no severed nerves, no paralysis, no brain damage, no broken leg/arm/hip/back…
2. This is just a CHANGE in your plans.
3. Work on how you're going to make the next three months fun and exciting, albeit different than you had planned.
4. More time for sightseeing, relaxing, writing, reading, singing.
5. So you'll miss some bike riding. You'll still get to see all these wonderful countries, just not from your bicycle saddle.

Hang in there. You have a LOT of people rooting for you.

The next day I wrote the following.

You can't imagine the turmoil I'm going through now. I don't even know what I'm feeling except disbelief that this really happened. I'm always so careful, not reckless at all. I'm mad at myself, sad to have to miss any part of this trip and glad I'm not worse off than I am, but extremely depressed.

Everyone has been great, but I'm helpless. Haven't even been off-route enough to know the ropes of traveling alone on trains etc. Oh, I'll manage. It won't be fun. I'm hoping to get on the TK&A staff in the interim.

It all seems so unfair but totally my fault.

All through surgery I was referred to as the "American." I don't have a name as far as they are concerned. No one has even asked. Made me feel real secure (sarcasm) when the anesthesiologist took his hand-held machine and beat it on his leg to make it work.

By the next morning I had received an email from Bess, and I wasn't expecting her reaction to my accident.

Date: 12 June 2000
Subject: Accident

Write to me and tell me what happened. I need to know what to tell Mom and Dad. I need to know the extent of your injuries, what kind of neck brace, etc. I get this call from Craig that you are in a French hospital, but nothing directly from you. Talk to me, girl, and tell me what happened. THIS IS MY MOTHER VOICE SPEAKING! You know me; I need to know details, etc. Take care of yourself and do what they tell you to do. Don't even be thinking of what to do next until you're able to do what they tell you to do now. And PLEASE BE PATIENT!!!!!!!!!!!!!!!!!!!! I will check email when I get home from work today. Love you and so sorry this happened.

I must have responded with "remain calm" because I received another email that went on and on.

Date: 13 June 2000
Subject: Accident

Don't tell me to remain calm. You are not to do anything strenuous for a long time until things have a chance to heal. Make sure you ask the doctors if you are allowed to even travel for a while. Any jarring on your neck is not good. And no heavy lifting or bending over or lifting bikes, etc. I can just see you trying to work alongside those other saggers, and you must not do that.

(I had mentioned to Bess that I was going to try to work for TK&A while recuperating. Shouldn't have said that either.)

Those fractures may be stable, but they are still fractures and will take time to heal. One doesn't walk on a broken leg after it's in a cast, and one doesn't do any strenuous labor at all with a broken neck!!!!!!!!! This is my STRONGEST MOTHER VOICE, SO PLEASE LISTEN TO ME. You must rest. Capish? Now that we have that straight.

I knew my little sister and I were close, but I had no idea she felt so strongly about mothering me. I'm seven years older (and wiser?).

Date: 14 June 2000
From: Bess

I lie awake in bed thinking of all kinds of stuff I want to tell you. You need to get a copy of your medical records before you leave the hospital. Should you even be carrying your luggage? Before you make any decisions about what to do the next three months, please remember that your health is your first consideration. I keep saying this because I care and it's very important to me that you take care of yourself. I'm your little sister, and it's my job to worry about you. Love my big sister, Bess

My first real day in the hospital soon became my new routine: call for bedpan, eat, write on my PocketMail, catnap, call for more water and start all over again. I wasn't allowed to move at all. At dinner the first evening, just as I was feeling sorry for myself because I couldn't feed myself soup lying down, in walked five of my buddies: Dr. Sharon, Willma, Margherita, Sockless Bob and Seattle Barb. They had rented a car and driven back to see me. I was overwhelmed that anyone would go out of his or her way to do that after riding all day. They brought my passport and smuggled in some cookies and chips. I immediately perked up and felt like the luckiest person in the whole world. They said they'd do my dirty laundry so it wouldn't smell or mold and check on my bike to be sure it was taken care of.

By the end of the first day in the hospital, I had also received emails from my Webpage readers by way of Craig. This was truly the highlight of my day.

To: Craig (and passed on to me)

I'm sure you are getting a ton of email, but I can't help but write a quick note to let you know I'm thinking of you and Al. (Well, actually, I'm sitting here crying about Al...) I feel as though we're all friends although we've never met. I can't think about how close she came to death or paralysis if she's fractured C1-C3. Please let me know when you have details of how she's doing. Noreen

Please let Al know that she probably has more people rooting for her than she knew existed. Robert

Please convey to Al how sad we are to hear about her accident. More important, we want her to know that there are lots of us out here praying for her. She is in our thoughts and prayers. "Go for it, Al. Hang in there! We're behind you all the way." Harriet

The news about Al is really devastating. But if ANYONE can apply positive mental attitude and strength of perseverance, it's Al. It is phenomenal that she can have an accident like that and yet write so clearly and coherently about what happened. Thanks for being our communications link to the trip. We appreciate all your hard work, and don't take you for granted at all. Richard

I have grown to be in awe of Al for her spirit, her optimism and her discipline. No matter how tough the day, she seemed to find time to keep us posted via her PocketMail and to find a way to get the message to you. My admiration for her stepped up several notches as I read the journal in the aftermath of her accident. I have an image of her lying in the hospital, busily typing her thoughts into the PocketMail. Please convey to her my best wishes and all the positive karma I can send her way. She will be in my thoughts and prayers. Norm

So shocked and saddened to hear this news. I have been reading her journal daily for months now and feel as though I know Al. Tell Al: an accident is just that: AN ACCIDENT, not to beat herself up over it. Sandie

My heart is so heavy and sad for you. Please know that you are in my prayers and thoughts. All things shall be well. You are a very BRAVE and WONDERFUL and WILD WOMAN! I am always amazed at how our lives can be altered in a heartbeat and how quickly we can bounce back and go on with whatever we need to do for ourselves. Thank you for all the journals: many strangers such as myself love them and feel that you are our friend. Be a good patient and happy healing and trails to you! Linda

You have touched many more people than you think, and believe me, you are in our thoughts and prayers. Reading your journal has been a "must" on my list because of your spirit and positive outlook throughout your "odyssey." When you were injured, a part of my spirit was hurt, too. Please follow all of the doctor's orders and have a complete recovery as soon as possible. Jon

Today when I opened the Webpage and saw "accident update," I got a lump in my throat. "Oh no, I hope something hasn't happened to Al." And then as we read the description of the accident, I got this sick feeling in my stomach. It was as though a close friend had been hurt in an accident, yet we've never met you and you didn't even know we were all lurking the background. The power of the Internet is truly astonishing.

Anyway, all of this is to say my wife and I hope you heal quickly and that there will be some hidden benefit from all of this that none of us can see. You are a very special person. Garry and Cozette

Please relay our most sincere get-well wishes to Al. As we've grown to know her through her Website these last six months, I have gained new insight into people. We follow Al's Website as well as another one. The contrast in attitude and personalities between the two is amazing. Al has the most amazing positive attitude, doesn't bitch and moan, and realizes that when life gives you lemons, you have no choice but to make lemonade. Often during my daily life, I think, "I can approach this one of two ways; which way would Al do it?" We wish her the speediest and safest recovery. Earl and Katherine

By the second day in the hospital, another Webpage reader, Julia, sister of rider Fred from New York, had put out a request on my Webpage for donations to help me get home, as well as return to the trip. I was flabbergasted. There were enough donations to pay my way home and back. I had never experienced the goodness of so many people before. I just lay in bed and cried, wondering what I had done to deserve all this.

Two choir members had sent their best wishes along with parodies on well-known songs. Those made me laugh in between all the other tears.

Al, make a speedy recovery and come back to us soon. You are irreplaceable. Thought this parody on 'Singing in the Rain' might cheer you up. Come back soon. Joan

SINGING IN THE RAIN

We're bikin' in the rain, and campin' in the rain.
What a glorious feelin', it's rainin' again.
We're soaked to the skin. Will Tim find a gym?
We thought it would stop, but it's rainin' agin!
Let the storm clouds chase everyone from the place,
We're sure to be campin' with rain in our face!
There's clouds up above, but we're so in love
With bikin' and campin' in the rain!

We plan to welcome you back with a parody written just for you. Hope you know how much we miss you, Al, and look forward to seeing you back soon. Sandy

HAS ANYBODY SEEN OUR AL?

Five-foot eight, a teacher great!
Never one to hesitate,
Has anybody seen our Al?

Sun-screened nose, biker's clothes,
Nutella jars where e're she goes,
Has anybody seen our Al?
Now if you run into a five-foot-two
Covered with furs,
Diamond rings, all those things,
Bet your life it isn't her!

But could she bike!
And could she sing!
Bikes like Lance and sings like Bing!
Has anybody seen our Al?

On the evening of the second day, four more riders visited me. They had been off-route, and when they got to camp and heard the news, they immediately got back in their rented car and came to see me. Dr. Helen, Mechanic Barb, and the tandem couple, Al and Steve, came back the next day with train and plane information for me. That was a big help for sure since I had never gone off-route and didn't even know where to start. More Web readers had called from the States, just to talk and boost my spirits or to put me in contact with Americans they knew in Paris. I was going to be OK. I'd get where I needed to go.

Never was I pressured by anyone to go home, just to consider all options. Craig wrote an email that really made me think though.

Date: 13 June 2000
Subject: Medical suggestion

I was talking to Scott today, and told him about your accident. He had a suggestion I think you should consider.

That is, to come back to the United States temporarily, and get checked out by a specialist who deals with neck injuries. That way, you'll have a more reliable, professional opinion on your condition and your prognosis.

This is not anything you want to take for granted. You'd hate to have something disastrous occur, and find out later it could have been avoided, "if only you had known…" Talk with Bess. Talk with your Idaho doctor. Consider this.

Scott quoted an orthopedic doctor he knows, making an analogy of the cervical vertebrae and the head, to a 'stack of dimes, holding up a bowling ball.' It's precarious. There are risks.

I don't mean to get you down, but I think this is something you should consider.

Dr. Helen, in her gentle way, explained that I'd probably heal faster if I went home, even for just three weeks.

I was trying to be upbeat and not go into depression. I had so many decisions to make then. The hardest was whether I should go home to recuperate and if I dare ask my sister if she'd take care of me, especially after making such a big deal about not coming home for any reason.

I finally got up the nerve to ask Bess if I could stay at her place and if she'd be willing to take care of me. She agreed, although she let me know in no uncertain terms that while on her turf, I was to be her patient and I would have to listen.

Do you have any idea how truly blessed you are? You have such wonderful and caring friends who were there to help you make a most difficult decision. (I know this was not an easy decision for you to make. Coming back to the States, I'm sure, was the last thing on your mind.) And this sainte of a sister who is willing to take you into her home knowing upfront just what she is getting into! But we must get one thing straight from the get-go. You will be on my turf, and when I suggest (notice not tell) to you what you should or should not do, please know that I am only thinking of your best interest. All my overreacting has always been with your health in mind.

Yeah, Yeah! She was an emergency room nurse in a big hospital in Ohio, so I knew I'd be in the best of hands. She even informed me that she was to be referred to as Ste. Bess because she had agreed to take care of me. Her words were:

I was informed that the way one becomes a saint is to be tortured in mind, body, and soul before becoming elevated to the status of sainthood. It is an arduous trek. Not that many people are elevated to sainthood because they can't handle it. Please spell saint as SAINTE. That's how the French do it.

And I hadn't even gotten home yet. You must understand that Bess and I get along great; we always have. We try to backpack and take camping vacations together every year or two.

She was relentless in her mothering. The next day I received another email.

You have no idea who you are dealing with here. I spoke to one of the docs at the hospital where I work, and he gave me the name of a neurosurgeon for an injury that high. I think it's the right decision, but one you had to make on your own. In the meantime you must try to get some strength back so the flight home is not so draining.

I'm already thinking how to keep you busy (this mind never shuts down). You can do simple things, like watch ME pull weeds. You can cook, wash dishes, and eat my cookies. I might even find some work for you to do on the scrapbook. Ste. Bess

My sister was keeping me in stitches actually. I knew she cared, and yet she wasn't being nasty at all. She knew she had to be forceful to get me to listen. I kept her informed and she fired back with more advice every day.

No need for a thrashing now that we have come to an understanding about who the boss is! Just kidding.

Sounds like the hospital personnel are outdoing themselves in getting you home. Tell them thanks from me. Make sure you spell my name STE. They use that abbreviation in France. I'm glad we have things to laugh about. My frustration level was getting in the red zone. I don't like feeling so helpless. I'm trying to get things lined up here on my end so there's no last-minute making arrangement stuff. Drives me crazy. You know, must be efficient.

And then the next email had me momentarily scared.

I feel like such a failure. I'm not sure I should tell you this. I don't want to set back any progress you have made so far, but sometimes it's best just to blurt it out. I couldn't save the Oreos. I tried my best, but Mike [her husband] saw them before I could hide them and now they're gone. I bought the Oreos just for you, but alas no more. I hope you still want to come stay with me.

I had come to think that this accident really did happen for a reason. This was the beginning of a whole new outlook on life for me. The generosity of people was unlike anything I'd ever experienced before the trip. I was overwhelmed. Another email from a Webpage reader said it all.

Please pass on my best wishes for a speedy recovery to Al. There must be a poignant quote someplace about taking unexpected turns and landing in a place or situation quite unexpected, and, with the perspective only time can allow, knowing you landed right where you needed to be. Egads, such deep thoughts for early in the morning…Lori

Eight days after my accident, I was released to go home, but this was the second longest day since the accident. I was antsy and just wanted to get on with it, but time stood still. The head nurse went out and got my plane and train tickets for me. When she returned with them, she said she would take me to the train station at 4:30. Oh, boy, I really was going to be released.

She ended up taking my stitches out about 10 minutes before we were to depart. When she took off her doctor's gown, she looked like she was dressed for a night on the town. I was escorted to her blue convertible sports car and whipped to the train station. I had to hold on to my neck as she went around corners. I was being treated like royalty. At the station, she bought me bottled water and found a young Frenchman to help me get on the train and settled. She even stood on the platform until the train pulled away. Again I was overwhelmed at the generosity of people who didn't even know me.

The French hospital personnel took excellent care of me, and I have nothing but good things to say about them. By the end of the week, the nurses and I were laughing a lot over our language barriers, but somehow we always managed to communicate enough to get the job done.

At the Paris train station, I realized I was all alone, feeling insecure and uncomfortable due to the heat. Now I had to find a taxi on my own, and I feared the language barrier more than anything else. I lucked out because my cabbie spoke English. I handed him the slip of paper with my hotel address, and off we went. I had to hang onto my neck again as he raced around corners just like the head nurse had done. Do all French people drive that way?

At the hotel, I was to meet up with three Odyssey folks who were off-route and just happened to be in Paris. Bruce had been sick since Baja and had gone home to recuperate. He had read my Webpage while he was home and contacted me via Craig. He just happened to be returning to Paris the very day I was released from the hospital. Kathy was there to meet him, and Sarah had just returned from visiting her husband. The three of them went out and got food for me, combed my hair, and kept me company for the next three days. I was due to fly back to my sister's just 11 days after my accident. I was going to take a cab to the airport, but Bruce and Kathy insisted on accompanying me. It was even Bruce's birthday. They secured a wheelchair for me, not that I couldn't walk, but they thought I'd be treated a little more carefully if I was in one. I really appreciated their help.

When I landed in Cincinnati, the stewardess wouldn't even let me off the plane until a wheelchair was available. I wasn't allowed to walk 10 feet. I was wheeled all the way through customs and clear out to my car. Kind of freaked out my sisters, Barb and Bess, to see me nonambulatory. So they assumed I was completely helpless. I wasn't, but couldn't convince them right then. They wouldn't even let me hold my small bag of personal items while getting into the car. Oh, well. I had to get used to it. I was to be catered to unmercifully for the next week until I proved to them that I really was OK.

CHAPTER 10

Home for Recovery: Downtime Frustration

June 23 to July 31

7,606.2 miles to date

"If I had been any nicer to you, I would need a second halo!"
—My sister Bess

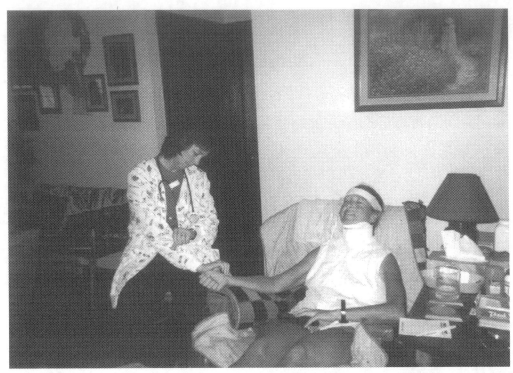

Bess nursing Al back to health

Al weeding Bess's garden by feeling out and pulling anything not in a row

10

HOME FOR RECOVERY

Bess had my little sick corner all set up when I arrived, including a recliner chair with pillows and blankets; and a table, complete with books to read and miscellaneous toiletry items that she figured I didn't have with me. I had come home with a toothbrush and the clothes I was wearing. My mom had donated some blouses, so I was in good shape.

All I wanted to do when I got home was sleep. But it only came in the form of naps. The neck brace dug into the back of my head, so I couldn't lie down or put pressure on my head for long periods of time. The back of my head, where the brace dug in, hurt worse than where my neck was broken. So I slept sitting up. I'd be up at 4:30 a.m. to read, eat, nap, eat, read, nap, all day long. I could never sleep for more than a couple hours at a time or stay awake for about the same amount of time. I was worried about getting really out of shape and fat. But my sister was relentless in her care. Being an emergency room nurse, Bess was in control, rightfully. It was her house and I was her patient, and she wouldn't let me do a thing for five days. I had to watch her pull weeds and I wasn't allowed to pick up anything weighing more than a few ounces. What a pain!

Soon after I got home (to Ohio), I received an email from Beth, on Odyssey, whom I considered to be a positive and upbeat person. But the stress was getting to her, too.

Date: 25 June 2000
Subject: You

We miss you SO much. We've had so many injuries lately. Even though no one is hospitalized, we are showing the strain of being on the road for six months and our weariness. We haven't quite recovered from the loss of you, Stan and Shirley. England is miserable cycling because there are NO shoulders, because traffic drives SO fast and because the roads are so narrow. The countryside is dripping with charm, but we are dripping sweat from raw nerves. That's a slight exaggeration. But we are a fragile group right now. I myself had several terrifying moments going through multilane rotaries in the wind and rain yesterday. I sobbed on and off all afternoon cycling in to camp. My euphoria with Odyssey lasted until London. The honeymoon is over. I am in a shift, and have no idea where the shift will take me. But I trust it will be to another good space. I think about you all the time. The disconnect with the ride, the discomfort of immobility, the frustrations of difficult decisions, etc. We are hungry for news about you.

LOVE, Beth

The fifth day after I arrived in Ohio, Bess took me to see a neurosurgeon. He gave me the OK to do whatever I felt like doing except ride my bike and lift heavy things. So I pulled weeds, one of my favorite chores, but because I couldn't bend over or see my feet or anything close to my feet, I had to squat and use the feel method. Anything not in the row was a weed.

We started taking daily walks on the local bike path, only a mile or so at first. Since I could not see where my feet were landing, I had to walk very slowly so I wouldn't trip. But walk we did, and I felt so much better. I walked around the yard several times a day if Bess was at work and I was alone. I hung clothes on the line to dry, again having to squat to grab the clothes. The neck brace was a very rigid plastic that allowed no sideways or downwards motion at all. I felt like a dweeb from outer space. But at least I didn't have to wear a halo. I had my sister's husband, Mike, haul their stationary bike up from the basement so I could ride during the day. I even typed on my PocketMail while riding the stationary bike.

The big bummer about my doctor's appointment was that he wanted me to have a CTT scan in another four weeks, and if all was OK then, he'd release me to return to the trip. That was great except that I had purchased a round-trip ticket and had planned to return after being home three weeks. So now I fretted over being stuck in Ohio longer than I wanted to be. All the more reason to exercise as much as possible to keep the blood moving and heal faster.

Plus I was bored being home alone so much. Bess and Mike both worked, so I spent many hours alone pondering my situation. In the evening, Bess and I would play cards or Scrabble and sometimes bake cookies. Eventually she started assigning me small jobs to do while she was gone during the day. I started receiving lots of mail from riders and Webpage readers, so that helped, too. Again I was hearing from people I didn't know, as well as Odyssey folks with whom I rarely spoke. Bess complained one day because I had received more mail in her mailbox than she had. Unbeknownst to me, Bess and Craig had been emailing back and forth to each other.

(They knew of each other before the trip but knew each other much better by the end of that year). I found out about this much later and just laughed.

Date: 28 Jun 2000
From: Bess
To: Craig
Subject: Non-entity

I'm beginning to feel like a non-entity. I opened the mailbox today and guess who all the mail was for? NOT US! I can empathize with you now more than ever.

Things are going well. We spent today shopping. Had intended to get an x-ray and her glasses fixed, and we were gone for six hours. Not only does she keep me out of the house and away from my housework all day, but she found the cookie can and is cleaning us out of cookies! Now that the doctor said she could do just about anything but heavy lifting, time to make her pay her way. There are plenty of weeds in the garden to pull.

Time to fix supper. Boy, does she eat a lot.

Ste. Bess

Date: 28 Jun 2000
From: Craig
To: Bess

Now that she's been released for light duty activities, I think you should send her back here to start handling the tons of fan mail, bills, banking, letters, cards, emails, Website, etc…

In the meantime, while you've got her, you might as well put her to work vacuuming, dusting, window-washing, car-washing, doing laundry, painting the house, fixing the roof, cooking, washing dishes, baking, mending, weeding, shopping, mowing the lawn, and anything else you can think of. That should certainly speed her recovery!

Have you got her on a stationary bike yet? How about swimming?

Slave Craig

Date: 29 Jun 2000
From: Craig
To: Bess
Subject: A new low

Well, I hit a new low at the post office today. While Her Royal Highness received several envelopes containing checks and adoring fan mail, I received only a flyer from Albertson's.

I tried to help Bess at home as much as possible, but the heat and humidity really bothered me. One day while she was mowing grass with the riding lawn mower, I swept off the sidewalks and raked a little grass. I sat in a lawn chair between jobs so as not to get too hot with my brace on. Bess kindly informed me, while I was resting in the shade on the deck as she drove by on the mower, that when one is not doing anything and the other is working in the hot sun, that it is expected that the one doing nothing (me) at least supply the one who is sweating in the heat (her) with a cold glass of water.

OK, I got the hint. So every half hour she was presented with a glass of ice water. Then once, while drinking the water, she looked at her watch and commented that we had missed lunch. I got the hint and presented her with a glass of milk and cookies from the freezer. Her comment was, "I could get used to this." She has always been the one in the family who could get away with saying things like that.

On July 10, a little more than four weeks after the accident, I woke up with excruciating burning pain in the back of my head. I asked Bess to take off my neck brace (I promised not to move) and look at it. This was the first time it had been removed since June 15. She told me it was quite ugly: wet, sticky and green. I panicked. I was sure I'd lose all my hair. And what was this, some infection? She put me back together and I fretted until she called from work and said I could get in to see the doctor that afternoon.

He allowed me to change to a soft collar that day. Yeah, no more brace digging into my head! My scalp could breathe, and I could wash the back of my head for the first time in more than four weeks (or rather Bess could). Only problem was he sent me to another doctor because he thought I looked jaundiced. They did some blood tests, and the doctor became concerned that I might have hepatitis because my liver enzymes were elevated.

This couldn't be happening to me.

I felt great except for the pain from the old neck brace. I didn't want another delay in returning to the trip. I was a mess. (I didn't tell a soul except Bess and Craig.) Of course, Bess, being a nurse, was worried about the rest of her family. Had I exposed them? Was it safe to let me cook (the one thing I could do really well)? I'm sure she was thinking in the back of her mind, "How much longer do I have to take care of her?"

I went into deep depression. I knew I'd been very careful on the trip. I'd had all my shots. How could I possibly get something like hepatitis? I kept thinking the green goo had to be an infection from the back of my head not being washed or getting any air. Seemed likely to me. Three weeks from this day, I had planned to return and meet the group in Sweden. I had three weeks in which to get well. I had already delayed my return and didn't want to have to do it again.

Bess started giving me more and more to do about this time, probably to help occupy my mind with thoughts other than possible hepatitis. My first traumatic job was to iron some shirts. Now let me tell you, I don't even own an iron. I buy gauze-like material that looks permanently wrinkled for most of my blouses, and my mom sews them for me. I just don't want to waste my time ironing clothes that will wrinkle as soon as you put them on anyway. I was thinking, "Gee, when was the last time I ironed, and do I even know which setting to put the iron on?" I didn't know how picky Bess was, but I'd never iron the shirts she gave me if they were mine. I did my best and fortunately got no complaints.

Then I was to vacuum. Now, I own a vacuum, but not a fancy one like hers. I was still groggy that morning when she rattled off how to use it, but I figured it out. That was more than I really wanted to deal with.

When we spent a day with Mom, I was supervising all the projects because I don't sew. No desire to learn either. Mom and us three girls were all working together, and they gave me a job of pinning things. I was doing OK, I thought, but was told I didn't even know how to do that, so they dismissed me and I took a nap instead. Boy, supervising was hard work.

While I was home, my journal entries became very boring. Let's face it: I was leading a dull existence. Not too much I could really do. So one day I decided to write and explain a little about myself so people would understand the comments I had made recently.

Date: 16 Jul 2000

I appreciate hearing from my readers, especially now while I'm not on the road with my Odyssey friends. I worry so much about losing my Webpage followers because there is just nothing exciting going on right now. I'm just sure everyone wants to hear about my daily chores (sarcasm), although some of them are not the norm for me.

So then some of you are probably thinking, "My gosh, she doesn't sew, she doesn't iron, what kind of weirdo is she?" Well, I'm one of those barely modernized people I guess. I still cook on a wood-burning stove, even though my new house has an electric stove and microwave, and I'd never owned a dryer until last winter when my renters bought one and installed it so they'd have it to use. They left it for me when they moved out.

I dig up my garden with a garden fork even though my dad gave me an OLD rototiller that is useless in my eyes. I've only used it once (or rather it used me). I lead a somewhat simple but good life. I just don't have every household gadget imaginable. No television, so no VCR.

I live out in the boonies, in the woods and sagebrush, bordering the Targhee National Forest. No lawn for me. I don't own a lawn mower. My "yard" is seeded in the natural landscape of the area. I weed-eat a path to hang up my clothes and for getting to the wood-fired hot tub. Wildflowers rule, as do native trees and bushes.

LOW maintenance. Gives me more time for hiking and biking. My organically grown garden is my pride and joy. No weeds grow there (at least not while I'm around), and I make my own compost. I do own a shredder for that purpose.

Another thing people don't understand about me is my philosophy about snow removal. I live in a heavy snow area. It is not uncommon to have 3 to 4 feet of snow on the ground at the height of winter. I do not own a snowblower. I clear my 750-foot long driveway by shovel. Half of it is too steep for a blower. (Even the local farmer had trouble the one time he tried to use the blower on his tractor—he was going to surprise me.)

I knew this when I built my house, but I've always shoveled and will continue to do so until I can't. For me it is relaxing and gives me a great sense of accomplishment. It is an almost constant job during the main winter months. I get done and start all over again. But think of the exercise I get. I'm outside in the fresh air, working hard so I can justify eating to my heart's content.

There is no time to watch television. I'll spend what little free time I have on the gorgeous sunrises and sunsets, or admiring my garden or driveway. Gadgets? Who needs them? Now you know the rest of the story.

There is nothing worse for an active person than to be forced to be inactive for any length of time. Sometimes our bodies force us to slow down whether we want to or not. At the time of my accident, I was overly tired. I knew it but pushed myself anyway. That was my way of living life to the fullest. Take advantage of every daylight hour. I had often said, "You can sleep when you are dead." But I don't think I had ever been as tired as I was at the time of my accident. Once I was forced to relax, I realized how tired I really was.

I had done nothing but eat, sleep, and read for almost four weeks and could still take naps daily. A big concern of mine was the muscle strength I was losing. It took six months to get where I was. It was frightening to think I'd have to start all over after a three-month hiatus.

I spent the next two weeks walking more and more, even walking to town and back, three miles one way. My niece couldn't believe I'd walk that far. I tried to keep busy and upbeat with positive thoughts that I would return as scheduled. It seemed that I started needing fewer naps, so I started thinking, "Maybe I'm back to normal now."

Bess and I took a weekend camping trip to Hocking County, Ohio. First time I had slept in a tent since my accident, and after that weekend, I knew it would be no problem once I returned to the trip. It felt so good to get out and do something different. We actually hiked, not just walked, with lots of hills and obstacles to watch out for.

On my final visit to the neurosurgeon, he said all was fine and I could return to the trip. No bike riding until I had another CTT scan in six more weeks. If all was OK then, I'd be able to ride and resume normal activity. So my next ordeal would be to find a doctor in Europe and get orders for a CTT scan. Not as easy as you might think. And I still had to be released by the "hepatitis doctor." He wouldn't check my liver enzymes until three days before my scheduled departure, so I just had to trust that all would be better by then.

The whole month of July was spent helping Bess pick, can and/or freeze produce from her garden. This was not a problem because gardening was my first love. There wasn't a day that went by in which something didn't need attention. I picked so many beans one day that Bess groaned when she came home because we still had to can them yet that night, even though I had already cleaned and snapped them. This was really the highlight of my five-week stay with her.

My last blood test had shown an improvement and although the doctor didn't release me, I wasn't sick and I could see no reason to stick around. In fact, my tests were almost normal. So I prepared to leave as planned. My neck felt better, although still stiff. I could not move it from side to side freely yet, but the doctor gave me exercises to do—and I did them faithfully. I could see my feet now, which was a great help, but I was still restricted in the amount of weight I could lift. So I'd be going back, having to ask folks for help with my heavy bag. I'd deal with that later, and I'd try not to be a pain.

About that time, Webpage reader Sylvia sent me a quote from writer Harriet Doer. I loved it.

Your Experience is Eternal

During your life, everything you do and everyone you meet rubs off in some way.

Some bit of everything you experience stays with everyone you've ever known, and nothing is lost.

That's what's eternal, these little specks of experience in a great, enormous river that has no end!

The best part about my forced rest period, or "downtime" as I like to call it, was the excellent care and companionship of my sister. We had some real quality time that I'll always cherish. There is supposed to be good in everything that happens, and being with my sister for those five weeks had to be the best thing that came out of that tragic situation.

Sisters are the greatest, and I have one of the best. Bess is one of those people who loves to shop for birthday and other special-occasion cards. Two of my favorites, that I've kept since she gave them to me, have verses that I cherish. My birthday card from 1999 contained a poem by Eva Allen:

What keeps two sisters close in heart?
It's the memories they share,
It's helping one another out,
It's showing that they care.
What keeps two sisters close in heart?
It's love and trusting, too—
It's the special kind of friendship
That they share their whole lives through.

On the other side it said:

Thinking of all the fun times we've shared,
The quiet times we've spent together,
And all the times we've helped each other through…
Thinking of all the ways my world is a better place
Because you are my sister…and my friend.

My birthday card from 2001 said:

What is a sister?

She's the one who dreams with you, grows with you, and shares with you the most precious moments in life.

CHAPTER 11
Europe:
Walking in My Tevas

August 1 to September 16

Walked 198.5 miles

"Buy some decent shoes. You can't be walking all over Europe in sandals."
—Laura Brattain

Charlie Hilliard walking with Al in a rural area outside Dresden, Germany

A house with flower boxes typical of rural Germany

11

Europe

Even though I was ready to get back to Odyssey, it was hard to leave Bess. She had been (and still is) such a blessing. She drove me to the airport and waited until my plane departed. She asked me later, why the delay? Yes, another delay. First it was a maintenance problem; then we were grounded due to severe weather in our flight path. I only had one hour and fifteen minutes between flights, and by the time my first plane landed, I barely had 10 minutes to board the second one. I flagged down one of those little carts in the terminal to get me to the gate on time. Talk about stress.

I was seated just as the doors closed, and the seat beside me was still empty. Some poor soul didn't make it. They told us that flight was completely full. We sat at the gate for an hour and a half due to backed up traffic on the runways. I could just see the fellow who belonged in the seat next to me, still inside. I was glad I wasn't that person. When we finally backed out to get in the take-off line, we were informed of an engine problem. Twice in one day? This wasn't making me feel very secure. So we taxied back to maintenance and were told it would be another hour to hour and a half delay. We were allowed to get off the plane, which was great. I had to let Linda and Charmaine know I was going to be late. They were going to pick me up in Stockholm, Sweden, and I sure didn't want them waiting at the train station for me. When I left the plane, first thing I did was look for a phone to send my PocketMail, then a bathroom. When I came out of the bathroom, I realized I hadn't paid attention to the direction from which I had come. I had no idea where my plane was parked because they had let us off at a gate other than the one at which we boarded. How stupid of me! I felt like a little kid who had been separated from his mom in a large department store. I told myself to remain calm. I had time, so I walked past each gate, looking for something familiar. You know, they really do look an awful lot alike. After a few minutes, I was home free. Whew! That was close.

When we were finally given the OK to leave, we were at least number 48 in line for take-off. That's how many planes I could count in front of us. It took us almost two hours from the time we entered that line to be airborne. I kept thinking, "We are flying across the water and two hours' worth of fuel is being used to taxi to the take-off point." Man, I hated flying. But I made it, six hours later than scheduled, and was it ever good to see Linda and Charmaine. As I walked to the exit area, I saw the back of what looked like another Odyssey rider. Couldn't be. But it was. It was Florida Bill, who was returning from visiting his wife. The four of us returned to our Stockholm camp with Charmaine at the wheel of a rented car. First thing Charmaine said to me was, "Al, you look great; you've filled out." I think that meant I had eaten too many chocolate chip cookies while recuperating. At least I didn't have that drawn look anymore. I returned energized and actually felt caught up on sleep. I was ready to go.

While I was at home, Cheryl had written and said I should get a purple scarf to hide my neck brace. So Bess and I shopped for the perfect purple material, and my mom made me a scarf. I wore it on the plane so there'd be no mistaking me. It was to become my trademark. Everyone knew purple was my favorite color, so that scarf became a conversation piece as well as a functional piece of clothing.

The best thing of all was the warm welcome I received from all the riders and staff, except for TK&A leader, Tim, who looked at me quizzically and asked, "What are you doing here?" I replied that I had written and said I was returning to the trip. Made me wonder if he was planning to send me home. I had been released by my doctor, and I had paid for the trip, so I was staying. It turned out that he was worried about me sagging with a broken neck. I'd been riding in a car all over Ohio; I couldn't see the difference there.

The day after I returned, we boarded a ferry to Finland. Eleven hours on the ferry gave me lots of time to reunite with everyone. We had choir rehearsal twice, played two games of Scrabble, and played Balderdash until it hurt to laugh. What a great re-entry day!

The next day was my first official sag, with many more to come while I was recuperating. The sag driver was instructed to stop 97 kilometers from camp and be available for ride support for the next few hours. I did not want to sit in a car that long, so I hit the road in my Teva sandals and walked 11 kilometers until another sag came along and picked me up. It felt great to be one with nature in the gentle rolling farmland. It was to become my routine for the next seven weeks. I chose not to walk on most of the rainy days. The only shoes I had, other than my bike shoes, were my Teva sandals, so that's what I walked in. I was too cheap to buy a pair of good walking shoes, even though I was severely chastised by my good friend Laura, from Idaho, for walking in sandals. Besides, I didn't have room for more shoes in my locker.

In the beginning, my feet hurt and got hot on the bottom. But as my feet toughened up, I was able to walk farther and farther. I started setting goals for myself to see how far I could walk in the time allowed. I loved it and knew I'd be in better shape for biking. It wasn't working the same muscles, but it strengthened me nonetheless.

Because walking was my only real exercise, I tried to walk a lot, even when I'd get to camp at the end of the day. I'd ask various friends to walk into town or go sightseeing with me. Just because of that extra walking, I got to know people like Peter, Win, and Judy M. a lot better. I even asked other saggers who weren't really sick to walk with me. And I started walking through botanical gardens and on beaches with Charlie, and into the big cities with Alan. I just tried to keep moving.

We had five layover days in Helsinki, which allowed those of us who were willing to pay extra to take a side trip to St. Petersburg, Russia. That was a good experience. I actually spent time with Priscilla, a cyclist who discovered a lump in Africa, went home for chemotherapy, returned to the trip to ride, went home again for radiation, and then returned to ride again. She is one tough lady. Certainly made my broken neck seem almost insignificant in comparison.

We flew out of Helsinki to Berlin. This was probably our best flight. There were no delays and all went well. Thank goodness, because I was not getting over my fear of flying with all that had happened so far.

Two days out of Berlin was a short day into Dresden, Germany. I walked the quiet backcountry roads with gentle rolling hills and even passed five recycling bins along the edge of the road out in the middle of *nowhere*. I was on an extremely narrow country road when five Odyssey guys came along. They all stopped to chat a bit and then took off, except for Charlie. He actually walked several kilometers into Dresden with me.

We talked about all the beautiful flower boxes that were so prevalent on almost every building we'd seen so far in Germany. Many homes in Germany, the Czech Republic, Austria and Switzerland had them. I made the comment one time that it looked like each building owner was trying to outdo his or her neighbor. A local told me that some towns have contests each year to see who can most beautifully decorate their house. I believed it. Not just houses, but hotels, light posts, rotaries and bridges were adorned with flowers. I wondered who watered all those plants every day.

Europe was a land of ancient buildings and towns with every available inch of land used in a practical way. The people obviously took pride in their country, and I was so at peace, enjoying their gardens up close. There were days when I thought it couldn't get any more beautiful, but it did. The Mirabell Gardens in Salzburg, Austria, as well as the botanical garden in Geneva, Switzerland, were the two most dramatic and awesome gardens I had seen all year. The vibrant reds, yellows and purples were far more gorgeous to me than the more pastel colors I remembered seeing elsewhere. They used these bright colors in geometric designs that just took my breath away. The houses in Austria were probably the most lavishly adorned. Every window had a window box of brightly colored flowers, even on the second story. Many houses seemed to have a theme because they hadn't just put flowers in the boxes—they were well planned.

It was while walking in Germany and Austria that I came up with the big idea to go home and promote flower boxes in my hometown of Driggs, Idaho, that next summer. I saw no reason why Driggs couldn't look like some of the Austrian towns. We had mountains in the background. How hard could it be?

Turned out to be pretty tough, actually. In February of 2001 I started that project, and it wasn't until a few days before July 4 that the flower boxes were in place, complete with blooming flowers. I had organized a few Boy Scouts and their leaders to help with the project, and what a job! I told myself to think twice next time before I tried to organize a project of that magnitude. But, hey, it was worth it. The town looked better, and lots of people appreciated it.

One of the highlights of Europe was in Salzburg, when Alan and I sang "Edelweiss" as a duet for breakfast that morning. After all, that was where the *Sound of Music* was filmed. Arnie asked me later that day if the choir had been singing a lullaby that morning. He said it was the most relaxing wake-up he had had all year. I was happy that our singing had a good effect on him. We hadn't intended to wake anyone up when we practiced.

I tried to walk every day in Europe. Once in awhile road conditions weren't the best, and I didn't put myself in situations where I might have to move fast—because I couldn't. I was really happy with myself though. I walked more and more each day and got up to 27 kilometers, roughly 16 miles, in one day. Many days I had been able to walk more than 20 kilometers, so I felt like I was getting my exercise and was still able to eat as I liked. Plus, I really pushed myself sometimes to get my heart rate up. The one thing I feared was losing ground and starting all over on my bike when I finally got to ride again. Some days I pondered for quite awhile before deciding not to walk because of conditions, but those days were few and far between. And I didn't feel guilty anymore when I made the decision to sag all day.

Because I had so much spare time, riders started bugging me to clean their bikes for them. Egads, I didn't even like to clean my own! Why would I want to clean someone else's? But I was getting offers of $10, $15 and $20 per bike. I knew how much time it took and lots of riders just didn't want to deal with it on top of everything else. (I didn't either.) But me, clean bikes? I thought they had gone mad. Some were relentless in their begging, and I finally gave in for $20 a bike. It took me an hour to clean the average dirty bike, and most were *really* dirty. It gave me something to do as well as some extra spending money. Charlie asked me why I cleaned bikes when I hated it so. I never had a good answer except that it was better than doing nothing, and I could help fellow riders.

The choir practiced as often as possible to make up for lost time. Our first real performance was in Geneva, Switzerland. Riders often heard us practice and continually bugged us for a concert date. (We had missed that promised London performance.) Now, I like to be prepared, and even though we were singing for fun, I wanted to sound good.

So our first performances were the same few parts of folk songs with a couple more added on. We decided to do a medley at the end of the year consisting of snatches of songs from as many countries on our route as possible. By the end of the year, we had songs from 14 countries, and we sang in German, French, Spanish, Italian and English. The basic theme of the medley was peace, love and brotherhood. The final medley that we performed at the end of the year started with "Love in Any Language," followed by "One World Built on a Firm Foundation" and "I'd Like to Teach the World to Sing." Then we went directly into the folk song snatches. The ending consisted of the songs "The Circle of Life" and "What a Wonderful World," with a reprise of "Love in Any Language" and "One World."

My job was to make the whole thing flow from one song to the next, nonstop, without having to start each song separately. I had to make sure each tune could be sung in the same key as the one that preceded it, or that we could modulate easily from one to the next. It was a fun challenge. Not only did I insist on the words being memorized, but we also learned harmony on many songs, and I had to come up with and teach the harmony with no piano for help. I loved it. By not being able to ride, I had time to sit and work on that.

The highlight of my day was when a cyclist-choir member would ride by singing and memorizing words, or when, in rehearsal, someone would say, "Can we do that again?" Oh, if teaching school could be that fun. I dreamed of starting a choir before I left home, and it became a fulfilling reality. When I think of Odyssey, one of my most cherished thoughts is of the choir.

Meanwhile, the PocketMail device had become very popular on our trip. Several riders came with them, and many purchased one after they saw how well they worked, so it was not uncommon to see several riders sitting together working on their PocketMail. On our layover day in Flims, Switzerland, I had some time before dinner to relax and asked Alice if I could sit at her table and do my PocketMail if I didn't talk. (That's what she was doing, and I knew she liked peace and quiet.) Then Ruth joined us and Alice proceeded to talk, so Ruth reminded her about her own rule. Soon Denise joined us and we had to go through the whole spiel again. It was quite comical since Alice was always the one breaking her own rule.

On our layover day in Zurzach, Switzerland, Charmaine and Linda and I went to a local hot bath. There were four pools of water with varying degrees of heat and all kinds of things to do. Dr. Charmaine forbade me to get in one pool because it had really fast water that whipped you around corners, and she thought it might be too rough for my neck. And that one looked like the most fun of all. But I was good and obeyed. It seemed like someone was always looking out for me.

Once I decided to clean bikes, there was often a waiting list. I had promised to clean several bikes the last day we were in the Netherlands, just before we went to Cologne. At the hotel where everyone was cleaning bikes, the only hose we had was the fire hose that came from inside. Imagine half a dozen bikes lined up along the edge of the parking lot with a cyclist at each one. Someone grabbed the hose and turned it on too far; the hose flew out of the person's hand and took off like a big snake. Meanwhile, everyone within 25 feet ran around, trying to avoid the wild spray while the rider who dropped it tried to catch it.

Later that day I picked up that same fire hose and promptly dropped it with the nozzle pointed smack at the front door of someone's tent. He had been cleaning it, and it was almost dry, but not when I got done with it. I felt bad. We were all so tired by that time that we just laughed. After all, it was only water.

Our last day in Europe was a layover day in Cologne, Germany. Charlie and I walked to the botanical gardens. Unfortunately, we exited a different gate than we entered, and since I had the map and was navigating, I was responsible for getting us lost. We walked off in the opposite direction of where we should have headed, but I didn't know it until much later when I could no longer find any of the street names on the map. I'm not sure how many extra kilometers we walked, but it was several. We had to ask for directions three times before we were able to get back on course. And through all that, Charlie was relaxed and never once made me feel bad. He was walking in biking shoes, and I knew that wasn't comfortable. Only thing he ever said was "Slow down," because I walked too fast. Yeah, I'd heard that before. My friends back home always said the same thing.

The six weeks we spent in Europe were some of the prettiest. I felt stronger than when I returned in Sweden. I had walked 198.5 miles and my neck was feeling pretty good. I was supposed to get a CTT scan in the Netherlands so I could get an OK to ride. But when I called the American medical contact in the Netherlands, he just laughed at me. Those kinds of things were scheduled months in advance, not weeks. I was bummed. So in mid-August I called a medical contact in Australia and lucked out with an appointment in Canberra. I had to have one in order to be sure all was OK, and believe me, by September 15, I was ready. My neck was still a little stiff, but I was confidant it was time to ride. As we left Cologne, Germany, my appointment scheduled for three days later was uppermost in my mind.

Just before we left Europe, one of my avid Webpage readers wrote a very nice email complimenting Craig and me. I've cherished it to this day.

One very important issue that needs immediate attention: Craig deserves a medal for diligent work behind the scenes on getting Al's daily journals posted. You're a hero, Craig.

Next: Al deserves a medal for positive attitude and perseverance. Where other Websites have dwelled on what TK&A could do better, Al is a living example that "Positive attitude is everything."

It was so nice to know that in September my Webpage readers were still following along.

CHAPTER 12
Australia:
The Neck Unveiling

September 17 to October 3

Biked 7,912.6 miles to date

Walked 262.5 miles to date

"My neck feels skinny and cold, but it likes the freedom."—Al

Al in the Blue Mountains of Australia

*Al with a "pineapple tree"
in Wollongong, Australia*

12

AUSTRALIA

Our flight out of Germany was delayed an hour. So what was new? We arrived in Canberra, Australia, 22 hours later, after having lost 10 hours in time zones during the flight. And because no buses were available due to the Olympics in Sydney, the riders rode their bicycles to camp. I walked those 10.6 miles and felt great.

Our arrival was one hour later than planned and since the airport was an Australian Air Base and not an international airport, we had to sit on the plane for two more hours until they could get organized to handle our group of more than 200 cyclists. They brought several people in just to process our entry into the country and were very thorough with agricultural items such as cheese and jerky. More than one of us had to turn over our snacks.

As we disembarked, dogs sniffed each passenger for drugs. Unbeknownst to me, one of my Scrabble buddies was a cannabis user. He had just purchased marijuana legally in the very liberal Netherlands and brought a couple bags of reefer with him. He got sniffed out, and they did a thorough search of all his bags. He told the authorities right where it was, but they checked every nook and cranny. Everyone knew that being caught with drugs was grounds for removal from the trip, so as of that moment, he was out. The staff wouldn't even allow him to camp at our campground that night, which I thought was a little extreme.

This fellow had wanted to go home from Europe, but I had talked him into staying. I kept telling him things would get better and that he'd come out of his slump. So I felt somewhat responsible. He told me later that he thought maybe subconsciously this was his way of getting to go home. He knew Australia had very strict rules about drugs. I felt so bad for him and for all of his friends. He was to be sorely missed.

As a result, Alan lost his regular roommate for future hotel rooms. It was at this point that Alan and I decided to room together so we could work on the talent show number we had signed up to do in the near future.

The next day I had my appointment for a CTT scan. I walked with Alan to the downtown area of Canberra only to find the hospital was clear on the other side of town. Canberra is rather sprawled out and it was 13 kilometers from our campground to the hospital. My appointment was at 11:30, and I walked in the door at 11:25, out of breath and very hot. I had to return in the late afternoon to get my results, and when they handed me the x-rays and a letter (which made no sense to me), I requested a visit with the reader of the films. He explained it was not his job to make recommendations concerning the x-rays. Great! Now what? He suggested I see a neurosurgeon. At 4 p.m. in the afternoon? What were my chances? The Odyssey group was leaving in the morning and I had to go along. I really needed to know if I could ride my bike. I pleaded my case and was able to get a "walk-in, wait and see if we can work you in" appointment. I did get in and saw a wise old man. He gave me his blessing to ride but said, "When you feel pain, it is trying to tell you something and you should quit for the day." Now how do you suppose he knew he should tell me that?

I returned to camp late because I took the wrong bus once and missed my last bus to camp by five minutes. I ended up walking part way again and made it in time for dinner. Instead of answering the same question 200 times, I took advice from Alan and held an unveiling ceremony for my neck.

I had missed choir practice, so at dinner we collected as many choir people as we could find. I just asked several if they'd come up and sing with me. They really didn't know what was going on. We huddled together while I explained what I wanted them to do. We ended up singing "Amen" three times and each time added one more thing. First it was harmony, then "Glory, Hallelujah," and then I ripped off my neck brace and the whole place cheered. Hugs, high-fives and camera flashes replaced the singing. For the past two months I had been known as "Ol' Whatserneck," but as of that evening, that name became history.

On my first day to ride in 14 weeks, I took off on a hiking trip, organized by Denise, into the Blue Mountains. I was so glad to get to go I even bought a pair of athletic shoes for walking the steep rock trails we were to be on for the next five days. That was sure to beat hanging around Sydney and all those people at the Olympics. I had no desire to fight the crowds.

Hiking in the Blue Mountains was definitely a high. I love to hike as much as I love to bike so hitting the trail in new country made me very happy. The terrain was different from what I was used to hiking back home. Here we had very steep cliffs to navigate, hundreds of stairs to climb at a time, paths carved out of the rock where you couldn't even stand up straight and so many unusual animals. The Blue Mountains are known for their poisonous snakes. We were told we didn't need to worry, but poor Denise was the first to spot one when she went off trail to find a secluded spot. We were very cautious from that moment on.

There were only nine of us in the group and not one was a whiner. We ate and hiked and hiked and ate. And my shoes were great. I should have bought them earlier in the summer, but

I was too stubborn. We had said goodbye to our gear trucks in Germany because it was too expensive to ship them to Australia. I no longer had to worry about getting all my stuff in that 17x17x34 compartment. We now used rented U-Haul-like trucks to carry our gear. I just had to make sure whatever I had could be stuffed into my bag. Eventually I bought another bag to accommodate my extra cargo and to divide the weight.

The hiking group returned to Wollongong in time to spend the last two layover days with the rest of the cyclists before flying out of Sydney. I spent one of the days visiting the Botanical Garden of Wollongong with Charlie. He found a tree with a yellow, trumpet-shaped flower that he just fell in love with. And I saw what I'd call exotic plants that I'd never even seen pictures of before. One tree looked like a huge pineapple. It was taller than me. I visited my first art gallery of the trip that day and walked barefooted on a sandy beach for the first time that year. It was there in Wollongong that I bought my very own Travel Scrabble game, too.

We flew out of Sydney and landed in Townsend. I finally got back on my bike—and what a thrill. All my doctor friends insisted I only ride half days at first, which I did. By the end of the first week I was up to full days of riding. I hadn't lost too much of my strength. Walking had paid off.

On one of our layover days in Cairns, I snorkeled for the first time. This was a real accomplishment, since I don't swim. A fellow cyclist, Krystal, held my hand while I was under the water, and boy, was it fun. I've been afraid of submersion since I was a young teenager, when I had to be pulled out of a swimming pool by a lifeguard. Just letting go of the boat was monumental for me. I had so many awesome friends on Odyssey who helped me overcome some of my greatest fears. I can never thank Krystal enough for putting up with me that day. I never would have done that by myself.

Due to some delay in our scheduled flight to Japan, we ended up with an extra layover day in Cairns. The choir took advantage of the time and practiced, even polishing the song "Leavin' on a Jet Plane" that was requested by the Odyssey media crew.

This crew, which was part of the staff, eventually produced four videos, mostly as documentaries but also for publicity purposes. Throughout the year, we were also greeted by newspaper photographers. Several Odyssey riders ended up on the front page of local newspapers. We were definitely news in the Third World countries.

The choir also polished a couple Australian songs just for the purpose of entertaining the restless Odyssey folks at dinner. Every time we had a flight delay, some riders would get really negative, so the choir tried to lighten the atmosphere with songs of the country we were in at that time. I had always envisioned the choir as an uplifting aspect of Odyssey, so we tried to promote harmony through song.

CHAPTER 13
Japan: Bus Bound

October 4 to October 11

Biked 7,912.6 miles to date

Walked 287.4 miles to date

"Try to slip down into an A- [personality] for a change."
—Alan Bouchard

Cheryl Minor showing her higher-strung counterparts how to relax

13

Japan

We spent an extra layover day waiting around in Cairns, Australia, and when we finally left, we flew to Kuala Lumpur, Malaysia. We separated into two groups and flew on two airlines to Osaka, Japan. I never did understand the delay out of Cairns. We were informed of a possible delay for the bikes on the day before we left and two days later, after spending a fun day sightseeing in Kyoto, Japan, we were informed that the bikes were not coming. So with our flights already booked, we embarked on a 10-day bus tour of the country. This was actually fitting because the Japanese seem fond of bus touring, especially in the States.

Our biking in Japan was threatened way back in July when TK&A announced a plan to omit that leg of the trip. So many riders complained that TK&A put it back on the itinerary. But once we were there, we still didn't get to ride. The problem had something to do with custom laws and the time needed for the application to be processed. Many riders were not happy.

Instead of riding and camping as originally planned, we rode buses every day and stayed in hotels more than previously scheduled (which added expense). After our tour, half of the riders were to be bused back to Osaka, the other half to Fukuoka, and we'd all fly to Hong Kong via Kuala Lumpur, Malaysia.

Some riders went ballistic. It was amazing how some just couldn't go with the flow. Several riders decided to stay in Kyoto on their own, some went ahead on their own to Hiroshima, and the rest stayed with the Odyssey tour. Of course, all these riders who decided to do their own thing did it at their own expense.

Rider Jim, who really wanted to ride 20,000 miles that year, was upset because the Japanese leg represented 500 miles he needed to reach his goal. So he bought a three-speed bike and rode by himself across the country. He did ride alone, but not on a three-speed. He found out later that first day when he went to shift on a big hill that he only had one speed. He made it, though, and Japan is NOT flat. He wanted those miles bad enough that he did what it took to get there. He then left the bike in the Miyajima campground. It had served its purpose.

We spent every day on those buses, averaging five hours at a time. We skipped a couple previously planned camps due to a 7.1-magnitude earthquake in one of the towns we were to camp in.

The campground in Amanohashidate reminded me of Baja. It was nothing more than a vacant lot with junk sitting around. We had five portable toilets and the TK&A showers. Definitely rugged, and that was right on the edge of a tourist town.

After a couple days, we decided to label one of the buses the "choir bus" and take advantage of all the time we had. For the rest of Japan, all choir members and their spouses and/or best friends loaded the choir bus first. Then those who wanted to listen to us practice filled the remaining seats. And practice we did, often for two hours or more every day. We made great strides in perfecting our medley and in learning new songs.

The bus rides also hosted marathon Scrabble and card games. Never were we idle. The countryside was very mountainous and visibility was often limited. On a bike it would have been great. In the bus, we just couldn't see much.

The campground at Mount Sambe was on the other end of the scale from the one in Amanohshidate. There was even a jungle gym on which to play. We arrived after dark and knew nothing of the facilities other than that we had good showers and toilets. The next morning after breakfast, Charlie, Margherita and I explored and found the jungle gym, which was wet and slippery from the rain, but that didn't stop us. We were crawling all over the equipment like little kids.

The leapfrog happened to be right near the cabin of a TK&A staff member and she leaned out the window and yelled, "Don't break your neck!" I yelled back, "Been there; done that." We never heard another word out of her. Once we had gone through all 10 jungle gym stations, Benj, Candy, Mark and Sandy joined us, and we went back through again. It was a great way to start the day. We were given two hours to visit Hiroshima the day we drove through. That seemed to be the story of our life that whole year. We spent hours standing in lines waiting at the airport but only had two measly hours to visit something historical. Delays prompted recurring complaints everywhere we went and became the main reason why many people signed off the trip to explore on their own.

From the time we left Cairns, Australia, until we arrived in Kuala Lumpur for that last flight to Hong Kong, we had ridden the tour bus for 27 hours and spent more than 60 hours either on the buses or airplanes, or standing in line to board them. That's a lot of time just standing or sitting in a week. We had very little time some days to even walk.

In my Webpage journal I always talked about the hours spent standing in lines and mentioned the adversities the group had to overcome, but I didn't dwell on it. My feeling was to make the best of what we had. Create our own fun. Amuse ourselves. And my group of friends seemed happier than most. A Webpage reader sent me a thought from Sigurd F. Olsen's book *Reflections From the North Country* that could not have been more fitting.

"It is one of the secrets of happy travel to see the humor that comes to the surface when it is needed, and is often the saving grace in what could otherwise have been a miserable experience. There is nothing worse than to travel with someone who cannot see the ludicrous in any happening. Nomads as we are, it is humor that may sometimes make the difference between life and death."

CHAPTER 14
China and Vietnam: What Are We Eating?

October 12 to November 9

Biked 8,601.7 miles to date

Walked 294.2 miles to date

"All you seem to do in recent days is ride in buses, trains, planes, etc...Don't you ride your bikes anymore?"—Craig Carpenter

Neil Van Steenbergen, Charmaine Jones, Peter Bolton and Al playing Scrabble on a train

14

CHINA AND VIETNAM

Flying into Hong Kong was the beginning of a six-week tour of Southeast Asia, and boy, was it different for me. I was introduced to squat toilets and trench toilets, a diet of dog and cat meat, more bicycles than cars, and more people than you can imagine.

After spending a day touring Hong Kong, we traveled by bus, ferry and bus again to Wuzhou. The normal local mode of transportation was the bicycle, and most bikes were outfitted with some sort of basket or crate. Cargo of ducks, pigs and dogs headed for market was very common. I had never seen anything like it before and wondered just what some of our mystery meals were. We asked some locals if they really did eat cats and dogs, and the reply was, "We eat anything that moves." I wasn't sure I was going to like that.

The choir ended up learning, and later, performing, three parodies on songs. The songs were very well received by the Odyssey gang, but we used discretion when we practiced and performed them. One was "How Much is That Doggie in the Hotpot?" to the tune of "How Much is That Doggie in the Window?" Those words were contributed by Phil and Joan of the choir. Another was "The Cat in the Kettle" sung to the tune of "The Cat in the Cradle."

Since toilets (or lack of toilets) had become an issue, Sandy, one of the choir members, came up with another parody on "There Must Be Fifty Ways to Leave Your Lover." We sang "There Must Be Fifty Ways to Flush a Toilet." Rehearsals were even more fun since we were adding choreography to this song. We tried to practice where no one would see us so that when we performed it would be a complete surprise. We succeeded in that.

Despite the new culture, major road construction with extremely tenacious red mud or fine red dust (depending on whether it had rained), and less-than-desirable accommodations, spirits seemed to be high. After all, we were in a geological paradise with many unique mountain formations. The 40 or so riders who had left the trip for six days to tour the Great Wall and other points of interest returned to Guilin, China, in time for our layover day. So there was a lot to talk about; we had a rest day in beautiful country unlike anything else we had seen up to that point.

I was having a particularly good time. The choir was coming along nicely. I had been riding with Charlie and Denise and spending time with several different riders. Life was good.

Bess and Craig were still making me laugh. I had told them soon after leaving Australia that I planned to treat them to an all-expense-paid vacation to somewhere, probably to Europe, to pay them back for all they had done for me those past few months. Bess replied with an email typical of her.

Date: 11 Oct 2000

I got a postcard from Craig. He went to Mt. Rushmore. He said he and I should have our faces carved in stone somewhere! We're discussing where we want to go on our all-expense-paid vacation.

And then three days later:

Date: 14 Oct 2000

Boy, oh boy, oh boy. That all-expense-paid trip to Europe looks better all the time. You'll never believe what I had to do this time. Do you remember that letter you had your French-speaking friend write to the hospital requesting a detailed account of the bill? Well, they sent it to Blue Cross—in French! So guess what Blue Cross did? They sent it to me and said this is all fine and dandy, but we'd like it in English, please. Now where on Earth am I going to get something translated from French, you might ask. Well, I thought of the French teacher at school. Then I remembered we have a book at work with a list of translators for almost every language on earth. I contacted one of the French-speaking ones, and she was able to translate it. Or at least get the gist of the message. Then I needed help with the money conversion (found that on the Internet) and asked one of the other French-speaking translators for help to make sure I didn't make a mistake. Then I wrote a cover letter explaining to Blue Cross that I did this to the best of my ability, but the message should be clear—even got the conversion rate for francs to dollars and told them what the bill was in dollars. (I sent the lady who translated the letter for me a potted mum as a thank-you.) That was a lot of work. But it's ready to be mailed. Just don't forget all those places you said you wanted to see again. You can show me next time!

I felt sorry for Bess and Craig for all the extra work and trouble I had caused. But neither of them ever really complained. Both kept their humor throughout the ordeal.

Date: 27 Oct 2000
From: Craig

Today I received the insurance check on the Odyssey 2000®, claim. What do you want me to do with it? Checking? Savings? Spend it on riotous living?

Date: 28 Oct 2000
To: Craig
From: Al

Riotous living? On whose part, yours or mine? Let's put half in checking and half in savings, and you go out to another show. Sorry this has been such a hassle for us all.

I felt so lucky to have a friend who just handled whatever came his way. I was hoping an all-expense-paid trip would be sufficient payback.

On our layover evening in Guilin, China, we had a big TK&A meeting to discuss the future itinerary. There had been lots of rain, actually flooding, in Vietnam. So what was new? But that was a major concern for a lot of riders. TK&A had been busing us through the soupy construction mud in China, so they were trying to accommodate us somewhat. It just seemed that long stretches of road (30 continuous miles or more at a time) were all torn up. And much of the roadwork was being done by laborers with picks and shovels. I never did see a piece of heavy equipment. I wondered how many years it would take to complete those projects.

It wasn't until three days after that fateful meeting in Guilin that I told the whole story. We were asked to not say anything on the Web, and I was still reacting and thinking that it was all a bad dream.

I finally sent the following email to Craig and Bess.

Date: 24 Oct 2000

You may not believe this and I wish it weren't true, but TK&A has announced that they are out money and the trip will end in Singapore. I can't even begin to explain the moods of the people or the trauma this has caused. For an additional $3,000 per person, Tim will continue the trip as planned. As a result of a questionnaire, only 23 people responded that they would be willing to pay extra to go on. We are in the process of having long meetings to determine the fate of this trip.

No matter what, I won't go home until Jan 1. I have my plane ticket [to fly out of Los Angeles in January] and I'm on vacation so am checking into many other options. Among them are spending a month trying to cycle Arizona with a friend, maybe trying to get a cheap plane ticket to Borneo for two weeks, who knows. At this time, there is so much anger, disbelief, frustration, internal turmoil and indecisiveness among the riders. We have all lost our umph. For me, New Zealand was going to be the highlight of my year. And if some go to New Zealand on their own on an inexpensive, round-trip flight, I might consider that. For me, I don't think paying TK&A is an option, at least not at this time. TK&A will see that we get back to the States from Singapore, so I won't be stranded in Southeast Asia, thank goodness.

To end in Singapore will be anticlimactic. Some of the best riding and best times will be lost. I'll miss the choir foremost. They are awesome for what little we seem to practice. And I'll miss my Scrabble buddies, singing with Alan and just living day-to-day with my newfound friends. I'm just not ready to give them up yet. I think we are all hoping for some alternative to ending in Singapore. That's what all these meetings have been about. Morale has just plummeted. I can't begin to explain all the options that have been suggested. We're just hoping to get to stay together until the end. We've been asked not to say anything on our Web pages, but I will eventually spill my guts to the world.

The next day I followed with an update.

Date: 25 Oct 2000

We voted on some options last night. Had about 19 to pick from and we each could vote for six. At breakfast there was more talk of creative ways to get to New Zealand. I saw the top seven responses this morning, and 126 people want to end in Singapore. Almost 120 voted to have TK&A somehow follow through as promised, but you can't get blood out of a turnip. I'm not giving up hope, but it doesn't look good.

Craig responded rather quickly, offering moral support as usual.

Date: 25 Oct 2000

Al, this is absolutely unbelievable. You bought a well-defined trip spanning an entire year, not just an open-ended trip until TK&A spent all your money. I'm sure it's *very* frustrating and upsetting for all. Good luck in dealing with this.

Less than a week later, Craig wrote to tell me we had passed the 80,000 mark in number of visitors to my Website since January 1, 2000. Wow! I really had a following. I even had readers write and ask me what all the recent talk was about. Several other riders had already spilled the beans, so one week after that first meeting, I alerted all my readers of the TK&A disaster. I wasn't revealing anything new—only the way I saw it.

Well, our big meeting to determine the fate of Odyssey 2000® was postponed until tomorrow. A few days ago we were informed by TK&A that money for the trip would be gone as of Singapore. Many options have been suggested by the riders, but basically, if we want to finish the trip as it was originally planned, we'll have to pay an extra $3,000.

I don't know where I am at this time. I don't want to miss New Zealand or Hawaii, but I don't feel like I should have to pay again for something I already paid for. What I do will depend a lot on what the majority of my friends do. For me, Odyssey has become the people first. Going home before January 1, 2001, is not an option for me. My balloon has been turned inside out, not just popped. After missing so much due to my accident, this is like adding the ultimate insult.

I'm still in shock that this has even happened. Ever since that first flight fiasco from Baja to Costa Rica, we wondered if we'd make it to the end. Why couldn't we have been informed earlier, like before the Japan fiasco? As a group we maybe could have come up with ideas to help the problem. The flights in Japan were so expensive and all those flights from here and yonder to go next door just didn't make sense. We've been told that excessive charter flight costs are to blame. So another night and day of turmoil, wondering what to do or what options TK&A might come up with.

The choir had been singing before each meeting since that first fateful one in Guilin, trying to lighten the mood. I wasn't ready to give up yet, although it sure was looking less than promising as each day went by. I just wasn't willing to dwell on the negative yet. I still had hope, and I wanted the choir to try to lift spirits if we could. At one meeting Alan and I sang "Feelin' Groovy" with choir back-ups on "doos" and "doots." We also featured Alan on "The Lion Sleeps Tonight" with choir back-ups on "a wem a ways." The choir was always well received.

Eight days after that fateful announcement in Guilin, as we were leaving China to travel to Vietnam, many cyclists had already made up their minds to go home early from Singapore. A few had decided to pay the extra $3,000 and go on with TK&A. The rest of us, myself included, were still in limbo. Coming up with the money was one issue and "What were the majority of my friends going to do?" was another. I needed to make that decision because it had been consuming all my energy just thinking about it.

I really wanted to go on and was leaning heavily toward paying the extra $3,000. I remembered my parents saying, "Just come home." Sorry, not an option! Craig and Bess did not try to influence me one way or the other, for which I was thankful. It had to be my decision, just like that decision I had to make back in June when I broke my neck.

So when I made my decision to pay the additional and go on with TK&A, I wrote home.

I have vascillated between frustration and resignation ever since we got the word from TK&A that the trip would end early without more money. I knew that night that Odyssey 2000® was over. The mood changed right then, people gave up and the forward momentum went right out of everyone. Tough decisions had to be made by everyone. Go home? Not an option for me, but it was for many. Hatred for TK&A flared. Disbelief and anger were common. The trip of a lifetime cut short by inefficiency on the part of the organizers was my take. I hated them for forcing us to make a decision we should not have had to make. Friendships were really starting to gel, and now we're being forced to part early. How to come up with the money on an already strapped budget? It just isn't fair. But what in life is?

It tore me apart to see my friends make decisions that took everyone off in different directions. I'll always regret this. But I can't go home early. That's not what I signed up to do. A few of my friends will still be here, but it won't be the same. Some refuse to give TK&A another penny. I understand. Some absolutely can't come up with the money. Some are tired and ready to hang it up. Some just want to spend the last month traveling on their own. Some are stubborn like me and refuse to let one more obstacle cut our trip short. It's sad, really sad, but you can be sure that we are all making every minute count. This is Odyssey 2000® and the adventure of a lifetime, and it will be what we make it.

I knew our time in Singapore would be highly emotional, but I looked at it as the end of a chapter, not the end of a book.

Those last two weeks in China and Vietnam were tumultuous. It had been hot, temperature-wise, as well as temperament-wise. Once my decision had been made to continue with TK&A, I was more relaxed and concentrated on having the time of my life.

Visiting Vietnam had been an education. The heat had been energy draining. Seeing how the people lived made me appreciate my home even more. And my visit to the Co Chi Tunnels awakened my memories of the Vietnam War era. It was beautiful country, geologically and horticulturally, and had been a great place to visit, but I doubted I'd ever return. I had enough memories of that place to last a lifetime.

CHAPTER 15
Thailand: Hidden Talents

November 9 to November 17

Biked 8,853.4 miles to date

Walked 296.1 miles to date

"There is no greater feeling than being onstage and having an audience go bonkers over you."—Al

Alan Bouchard and Al singing a duet on the Odyssey talent show in Phuket, Thailand

15

THAILAND

We flew from Ho Chi Minh City to Phuket, Thailand. Our hotel was one block from the center of the gay bar district. Wow! Another education. I asked Alan if he'd take me to a couple bars just so I could say I'd been there, and he willingly obliged. What a friend!

At one bar they were handing out free T-shirts that said, "PHUKET GAY FESTIVAL" in green, "Patong Beach November 9-10-11-12, 2000" in yellow, and a big 2000 in lavender, all on a dark purple background. I wanted one as a souvenir because it was beautiful and because those were the exact dates we were to be in Phuket.

Alan escorted me back to the hotel and then decided to go back out for a while. I asked him if he'd try to get me one of those T-shirts. He looked at me quizzically, and I said I wanted one "because it was pretty." When he returned later that evening, he threw a T-shirt on my bed and said, "I don't know where you think you're going to wear this." (It became a nightshirt.)

The choir had been practicing every spare minute. I still marveled at the riders who had been diligently trying to memorize their words. We were planning to sing those three parodies at the talent show and we really wanted them to be a surprise. Finding a secret spot to practice was often difficult, and more than once we crammed into someone's hotel room.

The talent show was held right after dinner on our last evening in Phuket and was the highlight of our time in Thailand. We had a sit-down dinner with waiters and fancy tables, but it was the worst meal of the year. We were served entrails soup (I did not eat that), and something that looked like fried baby birds (no bigger than the size of a large chicken egg). Those were just two courses of a multi-course meal served right before we were to perform. I ate very little, actually almost nothing. Many riders left and went out for pizza, then returned for the talent show. That meal wasn't what I wanted to eat before I sang.

The choir performed "How Much is That Doggie in the Hotpot?" "The Cat in the Kettle," and "There Must Be Fifty Ways to Flush a Toilet." The audience loved them. Then Alan and I surprised the audience with a five-minute medley of songs that contained the name of someone on the trip. For example: "K-K-K-Katy" for Katy, "You can get anything you want at Alice's Restaurant" for Alice and "Bill, I love you so" for Bill. We were told later that riders were anxiously waiting to hear a song with their name. We did 35 different names and just couldn't come up with songs for everyone. We were the hit of the show and got a standing ovation.

Absolutely no one knew about that medley because we always practiced in our room. Alan and I were on Cloud Nine that night. Neither of us could sleep, and I couldn't get ahold of Craig by phone. I found out later that Craig had gone on a bike trip and didn't tell anyone, not even me. The following was my email to Craig the next day.

Date: 12 Nov 2000
Subject: Talent show

No wonder you never answer the phone. I finally got a phone to work and you aren't there. Be forewarned, I'm going to call as soon after you get home as I can. Alan and I were the stars of the talent show, and I was on such a high last night I could not sleep. Took a bus today so I didn't have to ride on three hours of sleep.

You would like Alan. He's talented and fun, and boy, am I learning a lot from him. He's patient with me, just like you, although I'm sure he gets frustrated. His favorite line seems to be, "God, woman" and then on and on. He is not continuing the trip (out of Singapore) and that is going to be MAJOR SAD. I have had so much fun singing with him and seeing the world. He is a first-class world traveler and does a lot of things by himself, which you know I am hesitant to do. But, I am changing, I think. Hopefully, for the good. So when that phone rings after the 15th be prepared. I'll probably talk your ears off. If you have questions, you may want to make a list. I want to keep the call as short as possible.

That was an unscheduled phone call, but I felt I just had to talk to Craig. I had to share that evening with him because it was just so awesome. When I was finally able to call a few days later, I had forgotten about the time difference, and it was 5 a.m. his time. He didn't complain. But then I was all keyed up again and couldn't sleep, *again*.

The talent show was a definite morale booster. My congratulations to Kathleen for coming up with the idea and organizing it. I only wish we had done that several times throughout the year. We saw talents we didn't know riders had, including juggling and standup comedy.

The only bummer about the show was that several riders planned to go home from Phuket that next day. They wanted to avoid the sad goodbyes in Singapore. Some never said goodbye to anyone, and I was sad about that. I didn't even know until a week or so later that some had left.

That was how some felt they needed to deal with the end of their Odyssey trip. I could never have done that. I had to have a few hugs and maybe tears. I was counting on that.

A few days after the talent show, I just had to write to Craig again.

Date: 17 Nov 2000
Subject: Heaven

There's no greater feeling than being onstage and having an audience go bonkers over you. Boy, what that does for the ego.

I dreamed of an Odyssey choir from day one after signing up, and the great people in the choir made it a reality. This group has made my year. I am so proud of them and our accomplishments. I'm in heaven when conducting and instructing them. More fun than I can stand.

But the icing on the cake was singing with Alan, a real ham and excellent tenor. He can harmonize in his lower or higher register and knows words to almost any song. We have so much fun. When rehearsing for three weeks prior to the show, we'd laugh ourselves silly trying to get through our routine. The endorphines really flowed, and we felt so good.

But the response from the audience was tops. I felt like a real entertainer for the first time in my life. It was so easy being onstage in front of my fellow riders. Maybe this trip has removed some of my inhibitions. I'd like to think so. I give lots of credit to Alan who has had many years of experience in theater and musicals and helped to make me feel at ease. The choir will perform on the very last night of Odyssey in Singapore and will hopefully be remembered as one of the highlights of the year. It was for me. I get so excited when the choir responds to my instruction. That's what teaching is supposed to be like.

The main focus had been the talent show all during our stay in Phuket. But I'll always remember the geology of the area, too. Our three layover days allowed me to explore some of the natural beauty of the area. I snorkeled again; this time off a boat in rough water with Margherita holding my hand.

As we prepared to leave Thailand, the focus for me became preparing the choir for that final performance in Singapore and not missing one single minute with my friends who would soon be leaving. To heck with sleep. One of my favorite sayings had always been, "I can sleep when I'm dead."

CHAPTER 16
Malaysia and Singapore: Nearing the End

November 17 to November 26

Biked 9,279.2 miles to date

Walked 297.3 miles to date

"My Odyssey friends never did learn that nicety."
—Al, regarding bananas

Alan Bouchard, Margherita Kalman and Charlie Hilliard taunting Al with bananas

16

MALAYSIA AND SINGAPORE

When I think of Malaysia, I think of RAIN, RAIN, and MORE RAIN. It seemed we rode in rain, sometimes torrential downpours, daily. Sometimes it was a welcome relief from the heat, but mostly it was a big nuisance. We were told that November and December made up the monsoon season, and I believed it. Reportedly, one week after we were in Malaysia, they had major flooding.

The day after we took a ferry from Thailand to Malaysia, my Kansas friend, Fred, put out another plea on my Webpage, unbeknownst to me until much later, for Web readers to contribute toward the end of my trip. That was the third time that Webpage readers contributed to my Odyssey in some financial way. I felt honored.

Every day we had choir practice in preparation for the finale. During rehearsal four days before the concert, we were in the middle of a part where the choir hums (I had my back to the choir, mentally going over a speech I had prepared for that part), and one of the men started talking rather loudly. I wondered what he was doing and then I realized he was reading a speech the choir had prepared in my honor. It was touching and to this day when I read it, I become very emotional.

The Odyssey Chorus

The Odyssey Chorus will go down as one of the best parts of Odyssey 2000®. It's worth noting, however, that its history runs almost counter current to the ride itself, which began in apparent harmony with what seemed a shared vision and a distinct pathway to achieve its goal. By contrast, if there was any vision for what the chorus could achieve, it rested solely in the mind of the director, and she had to have a very fertile imagination. And so far as harmony was conceived, aside from a few obviously talented singers, the brunt of the chorus consisted of "wannabees" and "has beens." So, unlike Odyssey 2000®, the birth of the Odyssey Chorus was more discordant than harmonious.

But somewhere along the line things changed and the magnitude of that change will be graphically displayed in Singapore. While Odyssey 2000® will both figuratively and in actuality be preparing to fly apart, the Odyssey Chorus will be in perfect, well close-to-perfect, harmony. The singers will be listening to each other, supporting one another and caring for each other—a real team!

The credit for this transition lies squarely on the shoulders of our director, Al. It is your vision that brought us together and your myriad skills that have helped us achieve our success. You are a talented musician and a great teacher. You are honest but know when to temper your honesty to accommodate our exquisite sensitivity. You are patient yet demanding; resilient without being compromising. Your enthusiasm is infectious and your obvious joy at our success makes us try even harder. In addition, you are tough, courageous and a great cyclist. You are, in essence, a leader!

We in the chorus are in your debt and we want to thank you. We are not sure of your tastes, but we think we have something you will like. It also has symbolic meaning. It is an almost perfect circle signifying the unity and harmony you have created; it is bright and lustrous reflecting the joy the chorus has brought to both its members and its audience. Finally, there is a little sparkle which we hope will remind you of the sparkle in our eyes when, for the final time, we "flush those fifty toilets." We cannot thank you enough.

The Odyssey Chorus 11/21/2000

They gave me a beautiful gold bracelet. There were many tears, then laughter and hugs. I didn't know that the choir meant as much to the members as it did to me. And as the end rapidly approached, we made the most of every moment together.

All through Southeast Asia, few days went by in which Alan, Margherita, and I didn't play Scrabble and/or cards. Often Charmaine, Linda, or Charlie would join us. I guess we saved enough time not having to put up tents that we always seemed to have time (or made time) to play. The cards, Balderdash and Scrabble, as well as my music and pitch pipe, were the first items to go in my carry-on baggage on every plane, train and bus ride. I just knew I was going to experience Scrabble withdrawal when I went home in January. It had become a part of my daily life.

It also seemed that pranks were more prominent during the Southeast Asia leg. We had left all our camping gear in storage in Hong Kong since we were to have hotel rooms. Not having to camp just seemed to give everyone more time to play or think up things to do. Since I hate bananas, and always have, since I was a baby, my friends (?) took advantage of that weakness and tortured me. The first night I roomed with Alan, I found a banana on my pillow. YUK! The nerve of it all. I wanted to take a picture of Alan, Margherita, and Charlie on the train in Vietnam and when I had them pose, each of them held a banana beside his/her head. I found one in my fanny pack, in my DRG holder one morning, on my airplane seat when I returned from the bathroom, and under my pillow one night. I think Alan was 90 percent responsible, but Neil and Charmaine were in on it, too. Bananas are so repulsive to me that when Craig pulled out a banana to eat in my pickup truck on our first bike trip together, I pulled over and asked him to eat it outside my truck. Imagine the look on his face. But, when I'm at Craig's house now and he wants to eat a banana, he eats it in his bedroom, not in the kitchen where I would be eating. My Odyssey friends never did learn that nicety.

Malaysia was also the only place I ever rode with Alan. He actually rode slower than usual so I could keep up. Made me feel special since I knew he usually rode alone and as fast as the wind.

We took a ferry to Singapore from Desaru, Malaysia. That was the last day for all of us to ride as Odyssey 2000®.

I was still cleaning bikes in Singapore. I don't know why except that riders kept asking me to. But Singapore signified the last of "Al's Bike Cleaning Service." I cleaned three bikes that day. It's much easier to pack a clean bike than a dirty one. With everything else I was doing, I don't even know how I found the time.

The day we rode into Singapore we got together for the finale dinner, choir program and fashion show. That was not the usual fashion show. Several riders modeled their one prize acquisition of the year; others tried to be funny and come up with costumes. It was very entertaining and had a good effect on the mood of the group.

The choir medley was very well received. We enjoyed a lengthy standing ovation, and there were many moist eyes in the audience as well as in the choir. That was the last night of Odyssey as we had come to know it. Riders were scheduled to leave starting at 6 a.m. the next morning. It was so sad.

The next day was a layover day in Singapore for those who were continuing with TK&A to New Zealand. I spent it shopping, playing Scrabble and just talking with Denise, Margherita, Organist Bill, Alan and Charmaine. I was really trying not to think about my friends leaving.

But, alas, the time came all too soon. I accompanied Alan to the airport to say goodbye. I was going to miss him big time. He was a tease, a fun guy to be around and an awesome singing companion. I was OK until I got back to the hotel and sat down at breakfast with some other friends. I just lost it. And that was to be repeated several times that day.

After breakfast, Margherita, Charlie, Judy and I accompanied Ed and Willma by bus and train to the downtown area to say goodbye. They were two of the most upbeat people on the trip, and had become my confidants and riding buddies. I was to miss them dearly.

Charmaine and Linda left while I was downtown. We had said goodbye at breakfast. Then Margherita left just before I had to leave to fly to New Zealand. All those friends, some with whom I had spent almost every waking moment during the past six weeks, were suddenly gone. I was exhausted from saying goodbye and shedding so many tears. We promised we'd keep in touch (and we have, by phone, by email and in person). They were like family. When I signed up for Odyssey 2000®, I had no idea I'd meet such diverse, incredible people. Those friends and many others made the year the most awesome experience of my life. And it wasn't over yet.

CHAPTER 17
New Zealand: Looks Like Home

November 27 to December 16

Biked 10,353.9 miles to date

Walked 327.2 miles to date

"If you drove a milk truck and stopped as much as you do on your bike, it would be cheese before you got to where you were going."
—*Charlie Hilliard*

Al above Lake Wakitu and Queenstown, New Zealand

Al typing on her PocketMail in her Marmot Swallow tent

17

NEW ZEALAND

Those of us who paid the extra $3,000 to go on with TK&A flew out of Singapore on November 26 to Sydney, Australia. We had a 12-hour layover in Sydney and then flew to Christchurch, New Zealand, on November 27. There were 57 riders and 12 staff left, and fortunately, I still had several close friends on that leg of Odyssey.

Denise started a "weather pool" among Mark and Sandy, Jim, Charlie, Organist Bill, Ruth, herself and myself. We had to pick how many days we thought it would rain while we were there. It was late spring in New Zealand, so anything could happen. I voted for three days and Charlie voted for 11 out of the 19 we'd be there. Everyone else was somewhere in between. I was known as the "Sunshine Lady." I was thinking very positively at that time because I was sick of rain. (I wrote home to Craig months before, probably after Chile, and told him never to ask me to ride in the rain when I got home because I wouldn't do it. Period! No discussion needed.)

Anyway, the winner, the one who guessed the closest without going over, would be treated to as much ice cream as he or she could eat in one sitting, and the losers would pay for it. Hence, we became known as the "Ice Cream Gang." I like ice cream, but I could probably have counted on one hand the number of times I had bought ice cream during the entire year. The others, however, were ice cream fanatics. Most of them had been walking after dinner almost every night looking for an ice cream bar, regardless of whether they had already had dessert. I told them right from the beginning that if I were the winner, they'd all get off cheaply.

Now several took this weather pool rather seriously. We decided the first day that we'd vote every night at dinner on whether that day had been a rain day or not. Some, like Charlie, would consider a sprinkle rain because he needed 11 days to win, where others, like myself, would wait until they got wet to call it rain. Majority ruled.

Mark and Sandy were a tandem couple, so Sandy passed the day philosophizing to Mark on when rain was really rain. One night at dinner, the conversation among the group members started in on the philosophy of rain again. Sandy pointed out that a shower is not rain, but rain is a shower, likening it to the fact that a rectangle is not a square, but a square is a rectangle. I mean that was the topic uppermost on everyone's mind. Mark said, "Is this all we're going to talk about for the next week?" Some riders went so far as to threaten to soak tents with a hose to get people to vote a certain day as a rain day. The real ice cream lovers wanted to win.

New Zealand was everything I had hoped it would be. It looked like home (Jackson Hole, Wyoming, and the Idaho side of the Tetons). The weather was cool and more sunny than rainy. And the spectacular views rivaled those in Switzerland.

Neil and I rounded up Sandy and Patricia to be the New Zealand foursome for Scrabble. Even though we were camping again, we seemed to find time to play regularly.

One morning I was methodically taking down my tent, and after I shook it out, there was applause from a small group of riders (Neil and Organist Bill among them) standing near the gear truck waiting to load their gear. They had watched me dismantle everything, like it was their big entertainment for the day. I told them to get a life.

More than two-thirds of the Odyssey choir had gone home from Singapore, but I wasn't willing to let the choir die. Having taught 6th grade general music, I knew a New Zealand rhythm game that used lummi sticks. These are just sticks about 12 inches long, made out of 1-inch dowels.

On my way into Wanaka that first riding day in New Zealand, I stopped at a local hardware store and had them cut enough dowels for the remaining choir folks. I rounded up all the choir members that evening and taught them the first couple verses and challenged each of them to bring a friend to choir practice the next night. We could absolutely promise that no one had to sing. I would sing to provide the beat.

It was a game where you needed a partner. I challenged each new member to bring a friend until we ended up with 20 regular members. Some tried but felt that it was too stressful. That was OK. We'd need an audience eventually. Riders who had wanted to be a part of the choir previously but felt they couldn't sing jumped at the chance to be a part of the new rhythm choir. We even had several staff members in the group. That was such a unifying activity. We'd laugh and carry on like kids. We got to know the staff better than we had before, when they had so many people to account for. The new choir members wanted to practice as often as they could. I loved it. It was so fun to see adults having a good time over a children's game.

When we were in Rotorua, several of us went to a concert in which the locals performed with lummi sticks. Their game was more advanced than ours. I had hoped to have the new choir perform on our last night in New Zealand, so that concert was inspiring. And Organist Bill came up with the idea that if everybody in the choir made it through all seven verses without dropping their sticks, I'd eat a banana. I felt pretty safe on that one, but the thought was kind of scary.

When we performed, the rest of the riders were really impressed when we started throwing the sticks, and, yes, a few were dropped.

I rode with Charlie and Denise throughout most of New Zealand. One particularly typical spring day, while riding with Charlie, I seemed to have had to stop every few miles. It would rain and I'd need rain gear, then the sun would come out and I'd get hot, so I had to stop and take off layers. It alternated back and forth like that all afternoon. I couldn't stand to be hot, but I didn't want to get wet and chilled. So, Charlie, in his most patient voice, said, "If you drove a milk truck and stopped as much as you do on your bike, the milk would be cheese before you got to where you were going." Ha, ha! I suppose that's true, but I wanted to be comfortable. I just laughed.

I was so glad I had continued with TK&A. I still missed my friends who had left in Singapore, but they were still with me in spirit every day. I understood that some of them just couldn't afford to go on, and I was sorry about that. Those of us who did continue became even closer, and that took away some of the hurt.

On our layover day in Wellington, New Zealand, I shared a suite with Organist Bill and Charlie. We each had our own bedroom, and we had a huge common area with a small kitchenette. That was a really cool setup and one of our finest accommodations. We even had stick choir practice in our common area that night.

It was in Wellington that Charlie gave me the book *Zen and the Art of Motorcycle Maintenance*, thinking it might change my outlook on bicycle maintenance, etc. He just wouldn't give up. All year long Charlie had been very meticulous with his bike, cleaning and stroking it daily. Whenever we'd talk about bike repair or upkeep, he'd always say, "You can learn to do it." My response was always, "But I don't want to do it." I laughed hysterically at parts of the book because I'm exactly like the guy in the book who hates to do maintenance and can't understand the obsession of the other one, who is just like Charlie. I mean, that book could have been about the two of us. I did finish the book long after I returned home, but I can truthfully say that repair is not a skill I've learned. I'd still rather take my bike to a mechanic and pay someone to take care of it properly.

Charlie and I would have liked to have stayed in New Zealand and skipped Hawaii. New Zealand's weather was almost perfect. And how could the scenery get any better?

But we flew from Auckland, New Zealand, to Honolulu, Hawaii, and since we crossed the international dateline, we got to live December 16 over again.

CHAPTER 18
Hawaii:
A Blue Christmas

December 16 to December 29

Biked 10,551.1 miles to date

Walked 367.9 miles to date

"Reality is the leading cause of stress."
—Robert Jeffers, as submitted by Dave Hubbard

Alan Bouchard posing in a train station

18

Hawaii

As we flew into Honolulu, I realized that that was the last touchdown before the mainland. It was almost Christmas, but you would never have known it, looking at the city. There was no snow anywhere and very few Christmas decorations. I'd never been in a warm climate at Christmastime, and I had found it difficult to get in the mood.

At our first breakfast in Honolulu, the Ice Cream Gang had a meeting to discuss some technicality of the Rainy Day Pool. Our 19 days in New Zealand ran short due to some miscalculation, so Denise felt we needed to adjust the number of days each person picked. Before the meeting and any adjustments, I was the winner. The group came up with several options as to how to make it fair to everyone. Those options included adding the days before and after the scheduled riding days, adjusting everyone's guess by one day, leaving it as it was, or declaring me the obvious winner if I ate a banana split, which Charlie guffawed over. My friend Jim Higbee came up with that idea, so I questioned the validity of his "friendship."

It was unanimous that I eat a banana split and be the uncontested winner. Since I refused to eat a banana or anything that touched one, they relented and said I could have a Fudge Royale version with chocolate on top and no strawberry or pineapple. And I'd be allowed to pass the banana (and anything that touched it) to Mark when I was done. So everyone was happy, and they got to torture me.

On one layover day in Honolulu, Charlie and I walked to some "gardens" that didn't exist. We thought that we'd get to visit one more botanical garden, but when we got to the area it showed on the map, there was nothing there but a condominium complex known as the Gardens. Oh, well, we had a nice walk.

We flew to Kona, Hawaii, the next day and had another layover day. Several of us performed bike maintenance alongside the hotel. That was the day that Charlie and Organist Bill tried to teach me patience. We were helping each other prepare to enter the real world again, so we worked on a different theme each day. (Being a Type A+ person, I've always had trouble with patience.) I was trying to put new handlebar tape on, something I had never done before. Other riders walked by occasionally, offering advice and laughing at me while I tried patiently to accomplish that task. But I did do it by myself, and I was proud. It wasn't a pro job, but I learned enough so next time it will be easier.

We had another layover day in Hilo, Hawaii. And I did get to visit one more botanical garden, unfortunately alone. The next day I flew back to Honolulu by myself to play in Tuba Christmas, a program of Christmas carols played in four-part harmony by tubas and euphoniums (baritone horns). I was lucky to be close enough to participate, and that helped get me in the Christmas mood. While I was in New Zealand, I had made arrangements to borrow an instrument from someone in Honolulu, and I found someone to stay with for that one night.

The phone call I made from New Zealand to the organizer of the Honolulu program was unique. I had used a calling card and tried to explain as quickly and efficiently as possible who I was and that I'd like to play if they could find me an instrument. The gentleman that I was talking to wanted to chat, and I had to explain that we would be cut off when the time ran out (and we were). When I completed that call, I had no idea if the fellow even understood what I was trying to say. So it wasn't until I got to Honolulu that first day, when I called him again, that I even knew if I'd get to play. It all worked out, and I had a great time.

I returned to the Odyssey group for two more layover days in Kona. It was very warm, and I walked the 9 miles from the airport to the hotel in my Teva sandals. The black pavement was torturous on my feet. The heat literally melted part of the rubber on my sandals, and I ended up with the two biggest blisters I'd had all year, on the balls of my feet.

Our bikes were not available to us at that time because they were packed on trucks in preparation for the flight to Maui. Only about six riders kept their bikes out, including Charlie and Organist Bill.

By December 18, I had made doctor appointments and called my school, so the reality that Odyssey 2000® was almost over was very, very real. I knew I had to go back home, but I also knew I didn't want to go. I was being torn apart at the seams. I tried to stay upbeat and positive and make the most of every moment, but still the depression was there. The closer it got to Christmas, the more depressed I seemed to get.

I ate Christmas breakfast with Organist Bill and Charlie. We exchanged gifts, and Bill gave me a yellow harmonica shaped like a banana. My friends! They never gave up.

I wrote to Craig on Christmas Day about how depressed I was in that beautiful land of volcanoes and ocean.

Date: 25 Dec 2000

How is it one can be in Hawaii for Christmas and be depressed? I don't know how to answer that except it's just not the same. Here I go expecting Christmas to be Christmas as I know it, not willing to branch out into a new and different Christmas. But this is a very emotional time of the year for me. I miss my old friends, my horn playing at Christmastime, my dinner party, the Christmas as I know it. Here it seems to be make-believe.

I want to be with my closest friends, but they are off riding their bikes and mine is in Maui [with all the other Odyssey bikes]. I'm sure I'll play Scrabble with some other friends and sit by the pool, but it's just not what I wanted to do today.

I did have a nice long talk with Neil, a wise older rider who seems to have his act together. He understands my feelings, and I had a good cry. He, too, is feeling unsettled here near the end. The general feeling amongst the riders seems to be subdued, as was noticed last night at the party when many did not attend for one reason or another. (I went to church with Bill.) I think a lot of us feel a little lost right now.

Always the good and thoughtful friend, Craig replied with a really upbeat email.

Date: 26 Dec 2000

It's natural to feel a little down as you're coming to the end of your year-long vacation. But you're in paradise in the Hawaiian Islands! Take advantage of that. Go do something DIFFERENT. Find something you wouldn't normally see or do, and GO! Swim in the ocean. Walk on the beach. Soak up the sunshine. Go to a movie. See a play. Attend a luau. Take hula lessons. Sing something. Take pictures. Find a community band to play with. Have your hair cut. Get a massage. Buy a Hawaiian dress or long skirt. Eat pineapple. (Woops, I lost my head!) Write a song. Get your address book up to date for all your O2K friends. Eat seafood. Find a new game to play, besides Scrabble. Laugh. Go to the playground. Turn cartwheels.See you soon.

We flew from Kona to Maui after Christmas and had only one riding day in Maui, up Haleakala Volcano and back down. We spent two weeks in Hawaii and rode a total of only five days. It was like we were being weaned from our bikes.

We spent the next day flying from Maui back to Honolulu, then the next day from Honolulu to the U.S. mainland. We were heading home, and I wasn't ready to go.

CHAPTER 19
U.S. Mainland:
A Time to Say Goodbye

December 30 to January 1

Biked 10,798.9 miles to date

Walked 367.9 miles to date

"Tears are liquid prayers. Tears are the ice melting around your heart."—Shellie Rose

The Ice Cream Gang: Jim Higbee, Bill Garrett, Sandy Bovee,
Charlie Hilliard, Mark Bovee, Al, Denise Gilbert and Ruth Palombo

Al, Charlie Hilliard, Denise Gilbert and Jim Higbee on the last day of Odyssey 2000

19

U.S. Mainland

There were only two days left as we reached the mainland, and again an even deeper realization of the end of Odyssey 2000® set in. It wasn't that we kept dwelling on that; it was just so evident.

The best part of the last two days was getting to ride with Charlie. He had shipped his bike home from Kona and had planned to sag, but our leader, Tim, wouldn't let Charlie sag and gave him his bike to ride. I was glad. I learned so much from Charlie, including bike maintenance, patience and gardening ideas. We had shared lots of good times while cycling, walking through botanical gardens, eating and playing games. I knew that was going to be a tough goodbye.

On the second-to-last day, one of my good buddies and Scrabble players, Patricia, was T-boned by a skateboarder while she was riding her bike. She was knocked unconscious and ended up in the hospital for eight days with a concussion. A sad ending for her and her friends. We had no goodbyes and we didn't get to finish our Scrabble game.

Our dinner on December 30, better known as the "next-to-last supper," was a night to remember. We had my favorite food, Mexican, and I shared it with my favorite people of the trip: Charlie, Mark and Sandy, Denise, Bill, Neil, Benj and Candy. They were all a big part of my Odyssey family, as they were the people with whom I really bonded and felt most comfortable.

Upon our arrival in Los Angeles the next day, Denise met Charlie and me and told us about the ice cream payoff party. What a great time I had indulging in six of the most delicious chocolate Baskin-Robbins flavors. The rest of the ice cream gang paid my tab, and Organist Bill said, "It cost us $1.15 apiece for 17 days of fun." I had told them they'd get off cheaply.

New Year's Eve dinner was anticlimactic since we didn't all get to sit together. The dinner table was too small to accommodate all the family members who had joined some of the riders. And some just wanted to sit with others for that last Odyssey meal. I felt that the dinner was too formal and somewhat unnatural. We disbanded early and didn't participate in the New Year's Eve celebration. What was there to celebrate? We had to go home the next day.

The next morning we were up at 3:30 a.m., to breakfast at 4 a.m. and on the bus to the start of the Rose Bowl Parade by 5 a.m. Having to say goodbye to Charlie was the hardest thing I had to do all year. Charlie wasn't riding in the parade since he had an early plane to catch. I cried all the way to the parade start and didn't even want to ride, but I did and was glad that I did. On the bus Alice sat across the aisle from me and made some comment about my crying and that Odyssey wasn't over yet. I waved her off, but when I got home I wrote to her to explain that I had been upset because I had said goodbye to a really dear friend. I apologized for not being able to talk that morning. Her response to me was, "Boy! What a good friend that must have been who had you blubbering all day on our last day. That I should ever have such a friend."

After the Rose Bowl Parade everyone dispersed, and it was like the trip never happened. For the first time in a year, I was in an airport with no yellow heads (our term for Odyssey riders because we all wore yellow helmets) anywhere in sight. I realized I was on my own. I had to pack my bike in a box all by myself, which was traumatic, and the New Year's lines were atrocious at the airport. I kept looking around for someone I recognized, but there was no one. I felt like I was on another planet. And I fought tears all day. On the flight to Salt Lake City, I was so distraught the stewardess handed me tissues several times.

Craig met me at the airport in Jackson, Wyoming, where there was snow on the ground and temperatures in the single digits. When I walked out of the terminal, a blast of cold air slapped me in the face, and I realized, yes, that was the end of an awesome year. No more bike riding for another four months. It was time to readjust and go back to work.

My first tasks were to tackle the remaining insurance claims from my accident, organize my pictures, and start writing my book. I had planned to hide out for a week before returning to my hometown, to give myself a chance to settle in gradually.

Slowly but surely, life would return to normal.

CHAPTER 20
Home: Re-entry

January 2, 2001 to February 28, 2001

"We've outgrown our hometowns." Charlie Hilliard

Al with the map that her Teton Middle School students followed during her leave

20

HOME

The overwhelming feeling of responsibility upon returning home was enough to make me want to run and hide. I felt like I would no longer have that free spirit to do what really made me happy but would have to do what was expected of me. That disturbed me greatly.

My first three weeks at home were rough. I put off going to my house until January 8. I just couldn't make myself go there. I didn't want to see anyone from my hometown until I'd had a chance to accept that I really was home. So I stayed with Craig for three days, catching up on financial and insurance paperwork. Then I was off to my friend Mary's house to work on my book. When I finally drove into town, I thought, "Is this where I live?" It looked so familiar, yet foreign and totally uninviting.

When I got to my house though, my spirits lifted as I saw my beautiful place in the mountains. However, once my renters left that next week and I was left alone in my house, I immediately fell into a deep depression. I had been crying off and on for weeks, thinking about my new friends who were no longer with me every minute of every day. Everything I did, or looked at, or thought about reminded me of certain individuals.

One particular weekend when school was cancelled for extreme cold, I ended up crying buckets of tears. I had to go to school just to get away from the four walls that wouldn't talk to me. Soon after that weekend I received a couple phone calls from Odyssey friends, and just hearing their voices made all the difference in the world. That was the turning point for me.

I had visited my doctor the day I returned to the valley and was I ever in for a surprise! I had gained seven pounds (would like to think it was muscle, but I'm not so sure), my blood pressure was up to 140/80 (my usual was 110/70 when elevated and 96/66 had been normal). And my cholesterol had shot from 176 to 217. YUK! I knew my diet had not been the best, but I figured all the exercise would have balanced it out. Guess not.

So I went on a serious walking program and often found it difficult to find friends to walk with me because they thought I walked too fast. But, hey, I had to keep the blood moving.

On one of my walks I stopped in to visit a friend in the subdivision where I live. I just wanted to say "Hi," not really talk much. Unfortunately, she asked a question that opened up the floodgate of tears. Imagine the two of us standing in her garage, alternately laughing and crying, trying to come to terms with my emotions. She had had a similar experience during that year I had been gone when she and her husband sold their house in North Carolina and moved permanently to Teton Valley. So she understood what I was going through.

I was lucky that it snowed three times in the first week I was home. For me, shoveling snow is therapeutic, not only physically, but mentally. Just being outside doing physical work gave me plenty of time to reflect on the past year, wonder about the coming year, and try to put my life in some sort of order for the present. I seemed to be OK until I went back in the house, and then the tears would start all over again.

On January 15 I returned to my job as band and chorus teacher in the middle school. It seemed like I had been gone for a long weekend. Nothing had changed. Being busy at school was a blessing in disguise. It kept me focused and my mind occupied, at least while I was at school.

After that first week home alone, I wrote to some of my closest Odyssey friends. I felt I just needed that contact.

Hi everybody,

I've been lying in my bed unmotivated to get up and do anything, although I'm awake every morning at 3 or 4. Dumb!

I'm more depressed now than I was in June after my accident because I knew then that I'd be going back to Odyssey. But now there is nowhere to go.

I've had no problem cutting back on food. I have no appetite really, my tummy is in turmoil most of the time and it's no fun eating alone. I guess eating became a social thing.

And worst of all, I am having PocketMail withdrawal. Me, who never even liked to write before this trip, now I won't shut up! So I decided to write when the mood struck, usually every night and early in the morning. And poor Charlie has been the lucky recipient of my ramblings. He has replaced my 500 readers I used to get every day on the Webpage. He hasn't told me to go away yet, though.

Thanks for letting me get this off my chest. It helps to "talk" to someone who maybe understands.

I had written a Webpage journal entry after the first week at home entitled "Re-entry." I also sent this to my Odyssey friends.

Listed below are incidents that occurred in my first week at home. These are the bright spots.

OK, I get into Jackson Hole a little after midnight the night of January 1, 2001, and Craig is there to meet me. Somehow my luggage got there before me, so we just hopped in my truck and took off. Quite a shock, temperature-wise. Only in the single digits, and I was wearing only layers of cool-weather clothes that I had been carrying all year. I was a little bummed to see my bike box in shambles with biking clothes hanging out of the holes. I'd never had a bike box end up that damaged before. So my first worry was whether anything had fallen out and been lost. I had packed my panniers, biking shoes, dirty bike clothes and a small backpack around the bike thinking they would be extra padding. After checking the bike and doing inventory the next day, I confirmed there was no damage and nothing lost. Yeah!

Soon after I arrived at Craig's house that night, he handed me a key and I said, "What's that?" He replied, "House key, don't you remember?" OK, OK. I was suffering from lack of sleep and only thinking about a nice warm bed.

The next day while I was sorting pictures, I had to explain why I had a few shots of black holes or the floor. I always tried to ask people to not advance the camera after shooting a picture, but often I didn't say it soon enough. I explained that I just couldn't control everything. His comment was, "Boy, doesn't that sound like the statement of a control freak?" He was joking, of course, just teasing me back into the real world.

Late one evening while I was working on Craig's computer, I had a question for Craig, who was sitting at the desk next to me. I babbled away, but there was no response. He had tuned me out. I asked, "Aren't you listening to me? I'm sitting here talking to myself? This is not helping me with re-entry and being normal." He just laughed. Then later I asked, " Can I ask a question?" and he said, "You *are* trainable."

Every time I ever walked with Charlie, he'd always ask me to walk slower. I always figured I walked about three miles an hour and that everyone else just walked slower than normal. Well, on January 4, I walked 4.4 miles in one hour and five minutes. Craig said, "See why everyone's always behind you?" Hey, I had to walk to stay warm; it was cold out there (4 degrees Fahrenheit).

I went into my local Kmart soon after I got home because I knew where everything was, and I hate wasting time going up and down the aisles looking for stuff. Imagine my surprise and distress when I walked in and the entire store was completely different from what it had been. While driving to the store, I had prepared in my mind a route that I would follow to pick up exactly what I needed. I couldn't even find the departments. So I asked the first employee I could find to direct me.

When I drove my car through town for the first time on January 4, the first sign that jumped out at me was the LAUNDROMAT. Now how weird is that?

I found myself driving like I was on my bike. I had to stop to shed clothes once, and I kept looking at the road with cyclist eyes, mainly analyzing the hills and shoulders.

While working on my book at Mary's house, I needed a break and asked her if she'd like to walk the three miles to the post office with me. She asked, "Are you going to walk 200 miles per hour again? If so, I can't keep up." What was wrong with these people? I was starting to get a complex.

When I finally arrived at my house, I was overjoyed at the condition of my house and all my plants. My renter had done an excellent job and had even repaired a couple plumbing leaks for me. My only problem was that I felt like a stranger in my own house. I couldn't even remember where light switches were and couldn't begin to find kitchen utensils.

I'm dragging my feet as far as getting resettled. I don't even want to unpack my clothes. I need to let the wrinkles fall out, though, since I don't own an iron. I might be wearing lots of sweaters for a while.

Emotionally, this is tough. I miss my friends. In talking to Charlie, he said, "We've outgrown our hometowns."

For my birthday in early February, I bought myself studded tires for my mountain bike. I was in heaven. I could still ride my bike, and I loved being able to ride up and down icy hills. Charlie was the one who told me about studded tires, and he was very supportive. Craig had a different reaction, however. When I told him, he said, "Al, are you crazy? Can't you find something else to do other than ride your bike in the winter?" Not the response I was expecting.

It took a long time to get over being home alone. I made more long-distance phone calls those first two months than I ever did in the year prior to Odyssey 2000®. But my sanity was at stake. I felt I just had to talk to people, and I still needed to ride my bike.

CHAPTER 21
In Retrospect

"It's never too late to have a happy childhood."—Tom Robbins

Mark Bovee on swinging logs in Japan

Al leapfrogging in a campground in Japan

21

IN RETROSPECT

Odyssey 2000® was the best year of my life, and I have no regrets about any of it. If it were possible to go back and relive part of my life, that year would be the only one I'd ever consider. I'm sorry I broke my neck and missed some biking and time with my friends, but I learned a lot about myself and about the rest of the world. I discovered that contrary to what I learned in my youth, the majority of people are fascinating and trustworthy. Strangers and strange places are exciting, not scary.

My school principal said I'd come home with wanderlust and not want to stay in Teton Valley after I returned. He's partially correct. I do want to travel more, see new things, do new things and meet new people. But Teton Valley will be my home base. It is where my home and gardens are.

I've gained a new perspective on living even more simply than I did before Odyssey 2000® and on being even more independent. There isn't anything I can't do now if I put my mind to it.

Almost a year after my return from Odyssey, I mentioned some of my future plans to Craig as we were discussing how some people always seem to wait for the proverbial "burning bush" to tell them what to do. He said, in his most sincere voice, "You don't wait for burning bushes; you plant them." I liked that.

I'm a firm believer in living each day to the fullest. And if no one wants to go out and play with me, then I'll go by myself.

Epilogue

Upon returning home from Odyssey 2000®, I made a list of goals I wished to achieve and have, one by one, been making those dreams come true.

Accomplished already:

Biking self-supported across the United States, soloing part of the way (2002)
Retiring from teaching to work full time at a landscape nursery (2003)

Near-future plans:

Hiking the Haute Route from Chaminix, France, to Zermat, Switzerland (2005)
Hiking the entire Pacific Crest Trail (2006)

Within five years:

Working in Antarctica for a year
Climbing Mount Kilimanjaro in Africa
Leading bicycle trips in the United States or abroad

To read more about the Odyssey 2000® bike trip around the world, look up Al's daily journal on the Web at www.jhcb.org. Click on "Al Young, World Cyclist" under "Members" and read about the bike trip that inspired this book.

Printed in the United States
by Baker & Taylor Publisher Services